T0066857

REVISITING THE FOUNDATIONS

Building Our Lives on Christ

DR. KAZUMBA CHARLES

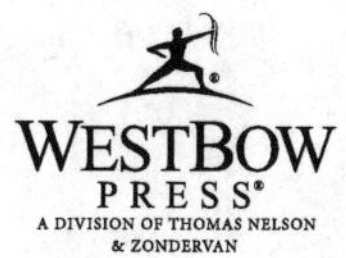
A DIVISION OF THOMAS NELSON & ZONDERVAN

WestBow Press books may be ordered through booksellers or by contacting:

WestBow Press
A Division of Thomas Nelson & Zondervan
1663 Liberty Drive
Bloomington, IN 47403
www.westbowpress.com
1 (866) 928-1240

ISBN: 978-1-4908-9754-7 (sc)
ISBN: 978-1-4908-9756-1 (hc)
ISBN: 978-1-4908-9755-4 (e)

Print information available on the last page.

WestBow Press rev. date: 09/30/2015

Contents

Dedication

I dedicate this book, first, to our Lord Jesus Christ, our strong and firm foundation. He has been faithful and good to us in every way. His precious Spirit has illuminated the Word of God in my life and given me a stable, unshakable, and indestructible foundation.

Second, I dedicate this book to the countless pastors and ministry leaders who have humbly committed their lives to teaching the Word of God to millions of people around the world at such a time as this. These men and women of God work hard to help people build their lives on the Word of God and on Christ, the foundation, in the midst of opposition.

Finally, this book is dedicated to Christians who desire to change the current spiritual conditions of their lives and of the church. The church is weak and powerless because we, the people of God, have become weak and powerless. Through God's powerful Word, we will be revived; and the present spiritual condition of our lives and of the church will be transformed so that once again we can become the light to the world.

Acknowledgments

I would like to acknowledge a most humble man of God, Dr. David Pierce of Faith Alive Bible College, and thank him for his impact upon my life during my time studying at Faith Alive Bible College. His wisdom, insight, and fatherly heart to the younger generation are extraordinary.

My special thanks to my beautiful wife, Glory Kazumba, and to the three children God has blessed us with for allowing me to spend more time in the presence of God and in His Word as I was writing this book. Thank you for your sacrifice.

To my mother, Juliet Kabwe, I say thank you for your great spiritual influence upon my life. Through your intense prayers for me, you paved the way for me to know the Lord and to serve Him passionately. Thanks also to my dad, Johnson Kazumba. Your love for people motivated me to love and help people in any way I can. May your soul rest in peace.

I also would like to acknowledge Jarl Waggoner for doing such a fabulous and professional job in editing this book. Jarl took my unpolished manuscript and turned it into a finished product with great dedication and wisdom. Thank you, Jarl, for making this book a success and for your valuable suggestions. You are the greatest editor I have ever worked with.

Endorsement

Let me say quite candidly that I was blessed and awed by the content of this second book by Dr. Kazumba Charles: *Revisiting the Foundations*. I believe this book and subsequent books written by people like Dr. Kazumba will bring to light the spiritual climate we live in today. I believe God has spoken to Dr. Kazumba and has put an urgency in his heart to write these words for every believing Christian.

Revisiting the Foundations is a great read filled with bold challenges. Written with a hold-nothing-back attitude, it will leave any Christian with a decision to make: either get serious with God and revisit your spiritual foundation or remain the same. It has certainly made me revisit my own roots of Christianity and my commitment to the Lord Jesus.

Apostle Terry Noel
Founder and President of Bridge Ministry International Inc.
Senior Pastor of the Saskatoon Full Gospel Church
Founder and President of the TEACH Bible Institute, Saskatoon, Canada

Foreword

Many years ago, my father and I visited the site of a beautiful house in our town. A house that was no more. Before that day's events, the house would have been anyone's dream home. Several times when my parents and I drove past it, I heard one of them comment about how beautiful it was. Although the house was relatively new, it was now in shambles. No, a Kansas tornado did not level it. Not even one of those strong Kansas winds had done the disastrous harm. The shock waves of a neighboring state's earthquake had not shaken it. So what happened?

My father explained that novice builders failed to build a solid foundation, so the house crumbled. Similarly, in the Christian walk, if our foundation is not solid, the storms of life, the earthquakes of emotional traumas or personal setbacks, the shaking sands of grief, or other shock waves of life can cause us to crumble.

In *Revisiting the Foundation* Dr. Kazumba Charles introduces us to biblical truths that can keep our lives on a stable foundation when challenges come. Dr. Charles also offers powerful insights to ignite the fire of a soul, to enrich the depth of a spirit, and to encourage even the most discouraged person.

The world is suffering from a lack of leadership and longs for direction. Because of that, the time is ripe for people to believe lies. People are more ready than ever before to accept the wrong kind of leadership. More eager to accept any philosophy, any teacher, and any "new truth" that flow into the scene. They crave inner peace, joy, love, and fulfillment but are turning to sources that leave them emptier than ever. All life's pertinent, political, and prominent issues . . . all the elements that stand as bulwarks of delusion . . . and all the pinnacles of man's proud accomplishments have mushroomed before us into an incredibly and indescribably empty world.

Amid the cauldron of confusion that exists in many minds, a new adventure awaits. Dr. Kazumba Charles's journey has uncovered some amazing insights about a hope, a help, and a hallelujah to be experienced by every reader of *Revisiting the Foundation.* You can discover, develop, and display a vital, vibrant, and victorious life as you incorporate these powerful insights from the Written and Living Word of God into everyday life. Dr. Charles introduces Jesus Christ, the Living Word, as the Key to living this new adventure.

As you read this amazing book, you will learn about the role of God as Father, Son, and Holy Spirit. You will discover heart-touching and heart-teaching truths in God's Word and learn how to make them real in your daily living.

Dr. Charles invites you to exchange a familiar faith for a fellowship faith. Every chapter of this book teaches a powerful principle of biblical insight to light revival fires in longtime believers and to nurture new Christians as they grow in their faith.

Dr. Charles has allowed the Holy Spirit to help him tell us afresh great biblical insights that invite us to a renewal of health, a realization of mind, and a realignment of soul that announce unquestionably to people of all denominations and all religions throughout the world that Jesus Christ is Lord and Savior to the glory of God the Father. The Living Word interprets for us the Written Word through the work of the Holy Spirit, glorifying God, our Heavenly Father. As you read *Revisiting the Foundation* by Dr. Kazumba Charles, you will discover renewed excitement about your faith in Jesus Christ. This book is a life-changing, life-challenging, and life-committing book that I recommend to everyone.

Dr. Wayne Norton, Executive Director
Hope Worth Having Ministries
Tyro, Kansas

Introduction

We are living in the most challenging, difficult, devastating, and overwhelming time our generation has ever seen. There is much talk of a global economic or financial crisis on the horizon. Deadly uprisings, civil wars, riots, and hunger plague the world, and Christians are persecuted and killed in many countries. And it appears these things are not going to stop anytime soon; rather, it seems we are going to see an escalation at all levels. The good news is that tough times do not last forever, but tough and well-prepared people do. Well-prepared Christians will stand the test of time, overcome every obstacle, and live for the kingdom of God, no matter what condition the world is in. The key to living for God in an ungodly environment is building a strong spiritual foundation.

Behind every social and spiritual problem stands the greater problem of the foundation. The foundation is the source of every issue of life, whether good or bad, spiritual or physical. Mankind has tried very hard to transform, reform, or change people and society but had little success, because the focus has been on the symptoms, not on the disease itself. Transformation is achievable, but it comes only by dealing with the root cause of the problem. That root cause is in the foundation on which people's lives are built for the foundation is the source of attitudes and actions.

God focuses on our heart because therein is the foundation of our lives. When the heart is corrupt, everything in us becomes corrupt. However, when the heart is pure before God, we live pure lives in the light of God's purity and holiness. Without the power of the Lord Jesus Christ and the Spirit of God, no person and no society can be transformed. We send thieves to prison; but after they have served their sentences, the chances are great they will return to the same life of crime unless they encounter the power and presence of God in their lives. Indeed, unless the presence and power of God touches and changes the very foundation of the lives of God's people and the church in general, they will continue to have a form of godliness without God and His power.

We Christians can come up with movements, programs, and laws to try to change the hearts and minds of people, but we will have no success until we allow the Holy Spirit to operate in our lives and let Him do what He does best: transform and change lives. Without the power of the Holy Spirit, it is impossible for us to make a difference in the world.

The problems the world is currently experiencing present a great opportunity for the church to rise up in the power and strength of God and become the anchor of peace, life, and stability in this unstable world. However, many Christians and Christian leaders are still spiritually asleep. They are waiting on God to do something, but God is waiting on them to act according to the power and strength He has invested in them through the Holy Spirit. Too many of us have prostituted ourselves to the things of this world and forgotten our kingdom call and mission here on earth. We look for things we can get from God, instead of looking for things we can do for the kingdom of God. God is calling on the church to wake up. He is calling on this generation of Christians to rise up in the power and presence of God and demonstrate the goodness of God's kingdom here on earth.

The troubling events taking place around the world are not only affecting the nations but also intensely affecting the body of Christ, God's people. As a result, the church today is experiencing a global spiritual meltdown. Passivity and apathy have overtaken the hearts of God's children. Many Christians are silently abandoning their faith and trust in Jesus Christ. False prophets, who seek only to elevate themselves instead of elevating God and pointing people to Christ, are springing up like mushrooms. The worship of God for who He is, is slowly fading away from many Christians' lives. People are worshiping God for His blessings and for what He can give to them rather than for who He is as our Father and Creator. Many,

many Christians have built their lives on a foundation of prosperity and not on the One who gives prosperity.

In many nations around the globe, it is slowly becoming an offense and even a crime to speak about the Lord Jesus Christ in public. This has caused many Christians to become passive, silent, voiceless, fearful, spiritually cold, and uninterested in the things of God. It is fair to say most Christians today are spiritually "hot" only on Sundays and within their church buildings, while being extremely cold outside the church walls. Where is that remnant of God, those men and women who are fearless and bold in bringing the presence and power of God to the hurting world? God is counting on His people to bring change and stability to this world. In every season and time, God raises up a remnant who will stand strong when everything around them is falling apart and breaking down. They become pillars of their nation and a source of hope and direction to the hurting world. Where is God's remnant in this season? Where are the mighty men and women of God of this generation who will rise up to proclaim the life-transforming Word of God and lead the nations back to Him? They are the people who are unshakable and fearless in difficult and challenging times. They fix their eyes on the powerful Word of God and on God's ability to do extraordinary things and not on the wicked environment that surrounds them.

The powerful people of God in the Bible who stood in difficult times and hostile environments and proclaimed the Word of God and worshiped only the Lord (Yahweh) had one thing in common: a strong, biblical foundation in their lives. Men of God like Daniel, Shadrach, Meshach, and Abednego refused to worship manufactured gods even to the point of death simply because of the solid, biblical foundation in their lives. They refused to allow their passing situations or environments to alter their belief in God or their love for Him. Sadly, today many Christians around the world have allowed the things of this world to shape their faith and belief system. And many more Christians are slowly becoming spiritually weak and unstable. In order for us to regain our spiritual position in the world and become strong in the Lord, we need to do one thing: rebuild the spiritual foundation of our lives.

Without a strong biblical foundation in our lives, it is impossible to stand against the spiritual forces and rulers of this world. We urgently need to revisit and reexamine our personal spiritual foundations if we are to stand strong in the Lord and against the powerful and evil forces of this world. The type of foundation we build our life, faith, and hope on surely will determine the strength and stability of our spiritual lives. We are stronger spiritually, mentally, and physically when we build our lives on the Word of God and on Jesus Christ, the true foundation.

Paul declared in 1 Corinthians 3:10–11, "According to God's grace that was given to me, as a skilled master builder I have laid a foundation, and another builds on it. But each one must be careful how he builds on it, because no one can lay any other foundation than what has been laid—that is, Jesus Christ." Paul here is simply declaring that there is only one strong, stable, and trusted foundation people can build on, and that foundation is Jesus Christ. Any other foundation is subject to destruction.

In Isaiah 28:16 the prophet Isaiah writes, "Therefore the Lord God said: 'Look, I have laid a stone in Zion, a tested stone, a precious cornerstone, a sure foundation; the one who believes will be unshakable.'" Isaiah is speaking of a foundation stone, a precious cornerstone that would be laid in Zion. This cornerstone is Jesus Christ, the Messiah. The foundation of the church and of all believers must be Jesus Christ. Jesus Christ alone must be our base, and everything we are and do must fit into the pattern provided by Him. Here is Paul's warning:

If anyone builds on the foundation with gold, silver, costly stones, wood, hay, or straw, each one's work will become obvious, for the day will disclose it, because it will be revealed by fire; the fire will test the quality of each one's work. If anyone's work that he has built survives, he will receive a reward. If anyone's work is burned up, it will be lost, but he will be saved; yet it will be like an escape through fire. (1 Corinthians 3:12–15)

Christ is the foundation, but we add to that foundation by building upon it what we might call our *spiritual foundation.* The foundation we have in Christ through faith in Him is essential, and it is the starting point for the spiritual foundation of our lives, which we build upon Him. We can build on Christ's foundation with all sorts of materials, but we must remember that on the day of the Lord, the fire of God will test and reveal what kind of foundation each one of us has been standing on. God knows exactly what kind of spiritual foundation each one of us has built. We can hide from each other and convince others that we are standing strong and building on Christ the foundation, but we cannot hide from the eyes of God. He knows where we stand and how we have constructed our spiritual lives.

Before God tests the spiritual foundation of our lives, Satan certainly will test it; in fact, he has already begun to do so. A person who has built a weak spiritual foundation will not be able to withstand the pressure and influence of the enemy. Only those who have built a strong spiritual foundation on Christ will be able to resist the Devil's influence and stand firmly on the Word of God. One portion of our spiritual foundation the enemy likes to attack is our faith in and faithfulness to God. If our faith in God is based primarily on God's blessings and not on who God is, as God Almighty, we will be defeated and give in to the enemy's influence.

If we look at the life of Job and Satan's accusations against him, we can better understand the concept we are talking about here. Satan accused Job of fearing and following God simply because God had put a hedge of protection around him, his home, and his property and had made Job prosperous in everything he did (Job 1:9–10). However, when God gave Satan an opportunity to test Job's motives for fearing God, Job proved that his reverence for God was not based on the protection and prosperity God gave him. Job feared God because of who God is: the almighty and all-powerful God. Job's life was built on who God is, not on what God gives; and as such he was able to endure Satan's testing without turning against God. His faith in and faithfulness to God were sealed and unbreakable, and in return God eventually blessed Job even more than He had before. A good and strong foundation can enable us to stand strong during the most difficult times of life.

Building one's life on the blessings of God rather than on God Himself is like building a house on a sandy foundation. When the blessings of God seem to disappear, can we still stand and worship God? Many people have given up their faith in God simply because their relationship with God was deeply dependent on God's blessings and not on God Himself. True faith and faithfulness to God's Word should be rooted in the character and nature of God. Can we remain faithful to God and His Word with all that is happening in the world? Can God count on us to become light to the nations, hope to the hopeless, and life to the lifeless?

Chapter 1

The Foundation

For any building, the foundation is critical. It must be deep enough, strong enough, and stable enough to support the weight of the building. Like buildings, we also have a foundation upon which our daily lives stand. In 1 Corinthians 3:9 Paul told the believers at Corinth, "You are . . . God's building." If we Christians are "God's building," then we must have a foundation. And the quality of each person's foundation will determine the quality of that person's life. In this book, we are going to revisit the foundations of our lives. God already has provided us the bedrock foundation of Jesus Christ. How we build our spiritual foundation on Him, however, is entirely up to each one of us. The questions each of us must ask ourselves are these:

- Have I built my life on Jesus Christ, the foundation?
- Have I built my life on the principles of the Word of God or on the traditions and doctrines of man?
- Is my spiritual foundation strong enough to withstand the pressures of life?
- Have I built my life upon the nature and character of God or upon my own character and desires?
- Do I desperately want to be spiritually healthy and vibrant?
- Do I want to change the current spiritual condition of my life and of the church?
- How can I stop doing things I do not like doing and bear good fruit?

Millions of Christians are rightly crying out to God for an outpouring of His presence! But do we have a foundation in place that can house more of God's presence? Many of us are trying hard to advance the kingdom of God but are failing simply because we do not have a spiritual foundation in place that will allow us to do so. Moreover, we desire change in our lives, but we are not experiencing long-lasting change because we have not yet established a strong spiritual foundation in our lives. That is why we "change" today but tomorrow go right back to our old ways and habits. The problem is in the foundation—at the very root, or base, of our lives.

The time is right for God's children to humble themselves and revisit their foundations. We cannot hide behind the veil of religion and play church while people are dying spiritually. And why should we continue to live without the true power and presence of God, which is available to us? Building a strong "spiritual foundation" in our lives is especially critical today if we are to live a powerful, stable, and unshakable Christian life in an unstable world. If we are to influence the world for God rather than allowing the world to influence us, our spiritual foundation must be strong and growing stronger.

The life of a true warrior for God is not easy. It is filled with battles, opposition, and challenges that come from the spiritual forces of this world. However, through the power of the blood of the Lamb of God, Jesus Christ, and by the word of our testimony, we can overcome all the challenges and obstacles we face. When we build our lives on Christ's foundation and on His character and nature, no weapon can prosper against us, and no spiritual force of this world can shake our faith and trust in Jesus Christ. Our faith in Yahweh and in His Son Yeshua (Jesus) is sealed, and nothing can change that.

The focus of this book is on the strength of our personal spiritual foundation and not on "doctrinal" issues. We may touch on some doctrinal topics, but they are not the focus of the book. The goal of this book is to help men and women of God stand on the undefeatable, unshakable, and indestructible foundation of Jesus Christ. Too many Christians are living in defeat simply because they are building their lives on a shaky and destructible foundation. Christ's foundation is solid, firm, and trustworthy. It is a foundation that no force or power in this world can move.

The biggest problem in the Christian world today is not doctrinal error, though that has contributed to the problems in the church. One of the biggest problem is finding men and women who are strong in the Lord, faithful, dedicated, and stable enough to save lives instead of watching them perish. Whatever our doctrinal differences might be, God is still focused on the mission of saving dying souls more than on anything else. To God, life comes first and above anything else. Jesus quoted from Isaiah 61:1 in declaring His life-saving mission to the world: "The Spirit of the Lord is on Me, because He has anointed Me to preach good news to the poor. He has sent Me to proclaim freedom to the captives and recovery of sight to the blind, to set free the oppressed" (Luke 4:18). And in Acts 10:38 we read that God anointed Jesus Christ with the Holy Spirit and with power so that He went about doing good and healing all who were oppressed by the Devil.

In the charismatic world today, we seem to be caught up in showing how anointed and powerful we are while not actually helping or saving lives. We have even gone so far as to brag about who has the best church and worship team, and, sadly, it is all at the expense of people who are dying spiritually and physically. We are wrapped up in ourselves so much that we cannot even see the will and plan of God for dying souls. The purpose of the anointing of God, the Holy Spirit, and the power of God in our lives is to save lives, not to provide an opportunity for boasting. So we will leave the issue of doctrinal foundations to other experts and in this book focus on our individual spiritual foundations and strength.

The stronger our spiritual foundation is, the more powerful and stable our life becomes. Maturity in the Lord and spiritual growth come by establishing a rock-solid spiritual foundation in our lives built on the foundation of Christ. In this book, you will discover the *importance* of building a stronger biblical foundation, one that can withstand any spiritual forces of this world. You also will discover the *means* by which you can establish or reestablish a strong spiritual foundation.

We Christians are in a spiritual battle, not a physical one. If we are to overcome the tactics of our spiritual enemy and not fall victim to his evil schemes, we need to be thoroughly equipped spiritually. We need to let the Master Builder, Jesus Christ, help us build a strong and unshakable spiritual foundation in our lives that will overcome those spiritual forces of evil and make us people God can use mightily to save and rescue dying souls.

God sets us free so that we can set others free. We are blessed to bless others, we are prospered to give, we are forgiven to forgive, we are rescued to rescue, we are loved to love, and we are lifted up to lift up someone else. Through strong, faithful, and dedicated men and women of God, the hurting people in this world have hope. Together we can make a difference in this world, but we must get our house in order and stable before we can take on the world for God. Unstable people cannot do stable things. God is consistent and steadfast in all He does; and if we are to work and walk with Him, we need to be steady and consistent too. And this is not possible if our lives are built on an unsteady foundation. Building a new and stable foundation will bring stability in everything we do: loving God, loving one another, and doing the works of God. God has given us everything we need to do His work; all we need now is to build our lives according to His plans and purpose.

WHAT IS A FOUNDATION?

A foundation is the lowest and supporting layer of a structure or building. In other words, a foundation is simply a base upon which something stands. This understanding of a building's foundation gives us a picture or illustration of what a spiritual foundation should look like and how important it is to build a strong foundation in our spiritual lives. Each of us has a foundation. Everything we believe in, everything we see, and everything we do is based upon it. If the foundation of your life is a godly foundation, you are going to be influenced by the things of God; but if your foundation is a worldly one, you are going to be influenced by the things of the world. Sadly, we have many Christians today who act like non-Christians. They have placed their faith in Christ, the true foundation, for their salvation, but they have sought to build upon Him a worldly spiritual foundation. You cannot be what you are not, and you cannot give what is not in you; you can give only what is already in you. And the only way you can change what is in you is by changing the root system of your life, your spiritual foundation.

Establishing or reestablishing a biblical foundation in our lives is an extremely important and serious step for every Christian. If it is not properly done, our lives will be shaky and unreliable and easily taken off course. A well-established biblical foundation, however, will help us stand in difficult times without losing our faith in God or being sidetracked in our walk with God. This is why Satan seeks to attack and destroy the spiritual foundation of every believer in Christ. If he can achieve that goal, everything else becomes an easy target for him. If the base of our life is dismantled, everything else in our life will collapse as well.

SPIRITUAL FOUNDATION

In this book, we speak of Christ as the bedrock foundation of every Christian's life. Apart from Christ, there is no hope and no stable foundation in life. However, we also speak of our *spiritual foundation.* This is what we ourselves build into our lives and on the foundation of Christ. We must first be sure we know Christ as the foundation of our lives; then we can begin to build that spiritual foundation that is grounded in the character and nature of God and in His Word. A Christian must build his or her life on the principles of Jesus Christ and on the Word of God. Through Jesus Christ, God has provided a strong foundation upon which each one of us can build a strong and meaningful life. He also has provided the Bible as a blueprint to help us build our spiritual foundation according to His will. In addition, He has given us the Holy Spirit to guide us through this process of building a spiritual foundation.

A life without God the Father, God the Son, and God the Holy Spirit is an empty, weak, and shallow life. God the Father, Jesus Christ, and the Holy Spirit provide us with a steady, firm, and fixed bedrock, which no person or thing can knock down.

If the foundation of our life is not properly established in Christ and built upon Him, our spiritual life can collapse and we can die spiritually. A poor and shallow spiritual foundation cannot withstand the floods, earthquakes, and tsunamis of this life. That is why we cannot emphasize enough the importance of building a strong foundation in our lives. If the foundation of our life is not properly laid or not strong enough to withstand the weight of life, the entire edifice of our life will collapse. A Christian cannot survive the attacks from the forces of this world or overcome temptations on a daily basis without having a firm spiritual foundation.

THE IMPORTANCE OF HAVING A STRONG SPIRITUAL FOUNDATION

We have already spoken several times of the importance of having a strong spiritual foundation. However, in order to grasp how critical this is, we must understand the spiritual nature of our lives and the conflict we are engaged in. Let us look at some truths from the Bible that relate to this subject. First, let us turn to Ephesians 6:11–13:

> Put on the full armor of God so that you can stand against the tactics of the Devil. For our battle is not against flesh and blood, but against the rulers, against the authorities, against the world powers of this darkness, against the spiritual forces of evil in the heavens. This is why you must take up the full armor of God, so that you may be able to resist in the evil day, and having prepared everything, to take your stand.

In these verses Paul clearly shows us why having a strong spiritual foundation is so important. Our battle is not against flesh and blood but against spiritual forces of this world. To withstand their tactics and attacks, we need to build a strong foundation that is equipped with the armor of God. The defensive armor Paul describes in verses 14–18 has five components, and he lists two offensive weapons as well. The defensive armor consists of the *truth* (belt), God's *righteousness* (body armor), *peace* that comes from the good news (shoes), *faith* (shield), and *salvation* (helmet). The offensive weapons are the sword of the Spirit, which symbolizes the *Word of God,* and *prayer* (prayer draws upon the divine, supernatural power of God).

The defensive and offensive materials listed by Paul in Ephesians 6 are very powerful tools we must utilize in our spiritual battles. When we are fully equipped with these tools, no weapon designed against us can prosper. The battle we fight is a spiritual battle that requires spiritual tools and weapons, and God has provided these for us so that we can face any challenge we encounter in our lives and do His work and advance His kingdom. Satan is not stronger than Jesus Christ is, and he is not stronger than we are when we are in Christ and with Christ.

In order for us to stand strong in the Lord and defeat the plans of the enemy, we need to be in Christ and with Christ and well equipped with the power of His Word. In 2 Corinthians 10:3–5 Paul writes this:

> For although we are walking in the flesh, we do not wage war in a fleshly way, since the weapons of our warfare are not fleshly, but are powerful through God for the demolition of strongholds. We demolish arguments and every high-minded thing that is raised up against the knowledge of God, taking every thought captive to the obedience of Christ.

Paul's statement helps us understand the fight we are up against and how we should fight it. Most of us try to fight spiritual battles according to our own flesh. We respond to spiritual issues with our own strength, wisdom, reasoning, and ability, and as a result we end up defeated. Moreover, when we try to counsel or help people who are struggling with spiritual battles, we do so in an unspiritual way and without even having a strong foundation ourselves.

Jesus said in Matthew 12:29, "Let me illustrate this. You can't enter a strong man's house and rob him without first tying him up. Only then can his house be robbed!" (NLT). Jesus is powerful and far stronger than Satan is. In the wilderness, He overcame Satan's temptations, and at the resurrection He defeated Satan's final weapon, which was death. Jesus' power to cast out demons proved His complete power and authority over the kingdom of darkness and all its forces. He alone is powerful enough to enter the kingdom of Satan, destroy, and violently take Satan's goods. (To "rob" in the above verse means to take with violence.)

Jesus Christ is a strong foundation on which to build our lives because He has overcome the kingdom of darkness. Having a strong spiritual foundation built on Christ is crucial, for our battle is not against human opponents but against the spiritual forces of evil in the heavenly realm. To overcome these forces and violently take what rightfully belongs to us, we need Jesus to be at the center of our lives. Through the Lord Jesus Christ, God has given us divine power to destroy strongholds.

One way we wage war against the forces of darkness is through prayer and fasting. The Bible tells us in James 5:16, "The intense prayer of the righteous is very powerful." Prayer is the most powerful resource we Christians have to pull down strongholds. It is through prayer that we defeat the plans of the enemy and his works. That is why we have to pray at all times and without ceasing (1 Thessalonians 5:16–18).

In John 18:10 Peter tried to fight Jesus' spiritual battle in an unspiritual way. He drew his sword and struck the high priest's servant and cut off his right ear. However, Jesus understood the nature of the battle He was in, and He responded to Peter's action by telling him to put the sword away. Jesus' battle was not a physical or natural battle. If it had been, He could have called upon His Father in heaven to provide for Him more than twelve legions of angels (Matthew 26:52–54). A Roman legion consisted of 6,000 soldiers. A roughly equal number of auxiliary troops supported each legion. Thus twelve legions of angels would be equivalent to 72,000 or even 144,000 angels, which would have been more than enough to defend Jesus against arrest and crucifixion. [1] Jesus did not call upon God to provide Him with an angelic army because the battle was a spiritual battle that needed a spiritual response. That is why He spent time in prayer hours before His arrest. In addition, of course, this battle had to happen in

---

1 Jeremy R. Howard, ed., *HCSB Study Bible* (Nashville: Holman Bible Publishers, 2010), 1848, note on Matthew 26:53.

order to accomplish God's will and plan for redeeming humanity from the powers of the kingdom of darkness, and that was not going to be achieved by the sword but by the power of the blood of His Son, Jesus Christ.

Most of us are like Peter. We try to fight opposition or circumstances with the "sword" of our mouth instead of going down on our knees and seeking the counsel of God. Prayer is essential because God's strength and power are manifested in our lives when we pray. God's power and strength make a difference in any situation. Many Christians are living in defeat because they try to use their own wisdom and limited power to fight spiritual battles. Jesus is the one who fights for us as we pray and stand strong on His solid foundation. All we need to do is establish a strong spiritual foundation through faith in the power and ability of God, faith in God's powerful Word (Jeremiah 23:29; Hebrews 4:12), and faith in the power of the Holy Spirit.

Living for Christ in a corrupt society requires a strong spiritual foundation in the Lord. The deeper and stronger that foundation is, the more strength we will have to withstand, resist, and defeat the Devil. Bigger things in the Lord call for a deeper foundation. We cannot attain higher heights in the Lord without properly laying down a foundation in faith, in the Word of God, and in prayer.

A strong foundation holds our lives intact and keeps us standing on solid and firm ground in the Lord despite surrounding circumstances. But we cannot build a new life on an old, weak, and unstable foundation. A new life must begin with a new foundation.

BUILDING A NEW LIFE ON A NEW FOUNDATION

We begin to build a spiritual foundation the moment we accept the Lord Jesus Christ and allow the Holy Spirit to influence and take charge of our lives. Unfortunately, however, many Christians stop building or developing their spiritual life right after saying a short "prayer of salvation." They seem to see the prayer of salvation merely as a passport or ticket to heaven and a way to avoid going to hell (*gehenna*). Instead, the prayer of salvation should be just the beginning of our long journey of building our faith and spiritual life in Christ. Other Christians try to build their newfound life in Christ on an old lifestyle or foundation. As a result, their lives do not change much, and they live as if they are not sons and daughters of the living God at all.

In Luke 5:36–38, Jesus answered a question of the religious leaders concerning fasting with this illustration or parable:

> No one tears a patch from a new garment and puts it on an old garment. Otherwise, not only will he tear the new, but also the piece from the new garment will not match the old. And no one puts new wine into old wineskins. Otherwise, the new wine will burst the skins, it will spill, and the skins will be ruined. But new wine should be put into fresh wineskins.

Most wineskins in the ancient world were made of goatskins sewn together at the edges to form watertight bags. An old and used wineskin was not effective for holding new wine because new wine expands as it ages, and that would cause the wineskin to break suddenly and spill all the wine. Jesus was saying the religious leaders of His day, the scribes and Pharisees, were like an old wineskin; they were stuck in their old ways, traditions, and rules to the extent that they could not accept or contain the new wine, which in this case was the good news of the kingdom Jesus preached. The powerful message of Jesus demanded a practical change on the part of these religious leaders.

The good news of the kingdom can be contained only in a fresh wineskin. In other words, our new life in Christ must be built on a new foundation and not an old foundation. The old foundation (heart or mind-set) naturally rejects the new ways and life that Christ demands of us as His covenant people. Jesus desires every human being who accepts His rule and reign to build a fresh and new foundation, or life, because the old life cannot accommodate the new life in Christ. The old foundation, or wineskin, prevents us from living a transformed life.

We cannot expect transformation to take place effectively in our lives if we continue walking in and doing the things of the past. Change is a process by which we move from the old ways of doing things to new ways of doing things. We have to be like new wineskins that can contain the Spirit and presence of God. We must be willing to scrap everything in our lives that does not help or improve our spiritual condition or empower us to do the will of God. Too many Christians are still holding on to the things of the past in their lives. It is time to move on and move forward with Christ with no turning back or looking back. The past is gone, and the new has come.

Paul writes in 2 Corinthians 5:17, "Therefore if anyone is in Christ, there is a new creation; old things have passed away, and look, new things have come." The apostle's point here is that true conversion begins life transformation, and this does not come by reforming the old nature. Many of us just want to reform our old nature, amending or changing it into an improved form. But God wants us to experience transformation, a radical change that alters our very nature and character. Transformation brings a change that captures our soul, mind, body, and spirit and leads us closer to the heart of God.

As Christians we are brand-new people who are recreated with the Spirit of God in us. "Old things have passed away," and "new things have come." The old things cannot be transferred into the new life in Christ but must stay behind as the things of the old life. Therefore, in building or rebuilding our spiritual lives, we are not simply to make a few changes here and there or just improve the old us; we are to let go of the old foundation so that we can clear the ground for a new and fresh foundation. A new foundation signals a new beginning and provides a platform for a fresh start in the Lord.

We cannot just rehabilitate our old life with the Word of God; we must allow the Holy Spirit to completely demolish our old life and the activities of it so that we can be new creatures recreated by the power of the Spirit. We must build our Christian life from scratch so that we do not have to deal with the same issues of the past all over again.

Many Christians are still dealing with the same issues they used to deal with or faced before they came to Christ because they have tried to build their Christian lives on a faulty and old foundation. A new foundation is what brings a new life. There is nothing more exciting when building a house than seeing a new foundation laid. Laying a new foundation will cause us to begin afresh in Christ and give us a solid ground for us to firmly stand on. A new foundation in Christ is what makes us unshakable in our faith and in our faithfulness in living for God. It is impossible to serve God faithfully without first establishing a new foundation. Romans 12:2 says, "Don't copy the behavior and customs of this world, but let God transform you into a new person by changing the way you think. Then you will learn to know God's will for you, which is good and pleasing and perfect" (NLT). In order for us to experience change and a new beginning, we need to build our lives on a new foundation and allow the Holy Spirit to transform us into new people with a kingdom mind-set. The way we think comes from our belief system, which is deeply rooted in the foundation of our lives. A new life in Christ calls for a new foundation.

THE JOY OF LAYING A NEW FOUNDATION

In the book of Ezra, we find something interesting in chapter 3.

> When the builders had laid the foundation of the LORD's temple, the priests, dressed in their robes and holding trumpets, and the Levites descended from Asaph, holding cymbals, took their positions to praise the LORD, as King David of Israel had instructed. They sang with praise and thanksgiving to the LORD: "For He is good; His faithful love to Israel endures forever." Then all the people gave a great shout of praise to the LORD because the foundation of the LORD's house had been laid. But many of the older priests, Levites, and family leaders, who had seen the first temple, wept loudly when they saw the foundation of this house, but many [others] shouted joyfully. (Ezra 3:10–12)

The Jewish people of Ezra's day, who had just returned from captivity, knew the importance of laying a foundation for the temple of the Lord. Fifty years after its destruction, they started rebuilding the temple. The celebration after laying the temple foundation was marked by various emotions. Some people wept out of joy, others sang with praise and thanksgiving to the Lord, and they all gave a shout of praise to the Lord because they knew a new foundation signaled a new beginning and a new chapter in their lives.

The laying of a foundation in our lives brings excitement and joy because it brings stability and assurance for our future. Indeed, the stability of our lives and our future is dependent on the strength of our foundation. The foundation we lay down today will determine the strength and longevity of our spiritual lives. A strong foundation will allow us to endure the tests that come our way without being shaken. Laying a new spiritual foundation requires us to dig deeply into the Word of God and to do what it says. To hear and do what the Word of God says is to build on a solid foundation. We all need a fresh start in our lives, a start that makes Jesus the center of our lives and the director of everything we do. We all need the Holy Spirit to empower us to live for God so that we can illuminate the glory and honor of our God.

The world we are living in today is unstable, unpredictable, ungodly, divisive, and filled with things that are designed to shift our focus and attention away from God and to ourselves. Because of this, many relationships among families and the nations of the world and even within the church have become dysfunctional. We blame everything and everybody but ourselves. We forget that change must begin with each one of us. When we change individually and fix our eyes on Jesus Christ, we begin to see things and people differently. The desire to lift and love oneself above anyone else suddenly disappears, and we become the source of unity, love, and hope to other people. Living for God in this unstable world requires God's people to have a new heart (foundation) and mind and the Spirit of Christ.

Sadly, most Christians are still standing on an ungodly, worldly foundation instead of standing on a biblical foundation. As a result, they do not love, forgive, and give as Christ does. We are called to emulate Jesus Christ. The reason we are not yet like our Master, Jesus Christ, is that we have not built our lives thoroughly upon His character and nature. Many of us have built our lives *around* the name of "Jesus" but have not built our lives *on* His character and nature. Building around and building on are two different things. To build *on* something means we are physically in contact with and supported by a surface; to build *around* something means we make a particular aim or ideal the main part of something.

It is sad to say that many Christians' lives have not yet made contact with the power and influence of Jesus Christ. All they have is an idea of who Jesus is and what He did for humanity on the cross. And based on that idea, they have built their religious foundations. That is not bad, but it is not enough if Christians are to forcefully expand and advance the kingdom of heaven Jesus preached. We cannot live for God in this world without letting the Spirit and power of God operate in our lives and transform us into the likeness of Jesus Christ. And there is no greater joy than that.

AN ENCOUNTER WITH JESUS

A true encounter with Jesus Christ brings a new attitude, mind-set, and character to our life. We do not become perfect, but we do become different from the way we used to be and act. The apostle Paul's experience on the road to Damascus in Acts 9 is a good example of a true encounter with Jesus Christ. Paul, called Saul then, was eager to kill Christians; but when he encountered Jesus Christ on the road to Damascus, his life changed, and so did his attitude toward Christians. Moreover, because of the influence and power of the Holy Spirit upon his life, Paul became a powerful preacher of the gospel.

No one can have an encounter with the Lord Jesus and remain unchanged in his or her spiritual condition. When Jesus touches our lives, we are changed. When we encounter the living and all-powerful God, He shakes everything in our lives that can be shaken, and He removes everything in us that does not produce good fruit. In addition, He prepares our hearts for a new beginning and a new future in Him. It is up to each one of us to put the past behind us and build our lives on a new foundation prepared by Jesus Christ.

> Forget the former things; do not dwell on the past. See, I am doing a new thing! Now it springs up; do you not perceive it? I am making a way in the desert and streams in the wasteland. (Isaiah 43:18–19 NIV)

When God delivered the Israelites from their oppressors, they were to start a new life. They were not to dwell on the past but to look to God to bring them home from Babylon through another "exodus," a "way in the desert," or wilderness. The point here is that the Israelites were to forget the former things and look forward to the new things God was doing and would do. Likewise, when God delivers us from the slavery of sin and the influence of this world, we must forget the things of the past and look forward to walking in the ways of God. Too many people seem to go right back to the old things they used to do after God delivers them. We need to let go of the past and embrace our new beginning in the Lord.

Another good example we can look at in terms of having an encounter with the Lord Jesus Christ is that of Zacchaeus (Luke 19:1–10). Zacchaeus was a chief tax collector, a supervisor of other tax collectors in his district. Tax collectors like Zacchaeus became rich primarily by taking advantage of their position and overcharging people. For that reason they were among the most hated people in Israel, despised as "sinners." That is why when Jesus said to Zacchaeus, "I must stay at your house," people complained and said Jesus had gone to lodge with a sinful man. But what is interesting in this account is that when Zacchaeus came into contact with Jesus Christ, his heart changed. He offered half of his possessions to the poor and was willing to pay back to anybody he had cheated four times the amount he had taken.

By giving to the poor and making restitution to those he had cheated, Zacchaeus demonstrated inner change by outward action. Moreover, his actions revealed that he too was a true son of Abraham. The point here is that a person cannot experience the presence and power of God and remain unchanged. Something in his or her life must change and reflect a changed life. The evidence of inner change is loving, compassionate outward actions or fruits. The change Christ brings into our lives must be visible to people through our attitudes, character, and actions.

Only a person who has been transformed by the power of the presence of God will humble himself and make things right with God and with man. Zacchaeus did exactly that. He felt the impact of Jesus' presence, and he responded by humbling himself before Him and by making things right with others. Jesus declared that salvation had come to Zacchaeus and his entire household that day. The magnificent powers of the Holy Spirit will cause us not only to make peace with God but also to make peace with man. Walking in peace with God and with each other gives clear evidence that the Spirit of God dwells in us.

A person who has truly experienced inner change will produce outward, visible results, or fruit. If the Spirit of God is dominant in our lives, we will definitely produce good things. According to John 7:38, a person who believes in Jesus Christ will have streams of living water flowing from deep within him. This "living water" is a reference to the Holy Spirit (verse 39). If the "living water" in this particular scripture refers to the Holy Spirit, then "rivers of living water" may mean the fruit of the Spirit or the life of the Spirit that flows from within a believer's heart or life.

IDENTIFIED BY OUR FRUIT

Jesus said, "A tree is identified by its fruit. Make a tree good, and its fruit will be good. Make a tree bad, and its fruit will be bad" (Matthew 12:33 NLT). The Pharisees of Jesus' day portrayed themselves as righteous (good trees), but their actions, attitudes, and words exposed the true nature of their hearts. Jesus here compared them to a bad tree with bad fruit because a good tree cannot produce bad fruit. The same applies to us today. If the foundation of our lives is built on Jesus Christ, we will produce the attitude, character, and nature of Christ. A worldly foundation produces the things of this world. A godly foundation produces the things of the Spirit, or the things of God. No one can say his or her life is built on Christ and yet continue to be influenced by the spirit of this world. In order to change a bad tree into one that produces good fruit, the root system has to be cut off and replaced with good roots. So, for us to change our present spiritual condition, we need to change the basis or foundation upon which our lives are built. Otherwise, we will find ourselves merely playing religious games that impress man but displease God.

Our knowledge, wisdom, character, attitudes, and actions display the core of our very being. Out of the abundance of the "foundation" of our lives, our mouths speak. To change what we are and become what God wants us to be, we need to change the foundation of our lives. Remember that the type of foundation we lay down will determine the design and structure of our building, as well as the strength of that building. Change comes when we give God access to who we are and allow Him through His Word to bring transformation to our lives. That means *our* knowledge, wisdom, character, and attitudes must go, and we must take up *His* knowledge, wisdom, character, and nature. Show me a person who is strong in faith, stable in the Lord, and full of the wisdom and character of God, and I will show you a person who has built his or her spiritual foundation on the wisdom, knowledge, and character of Jesus Christ.

Shadrach, Meshach, and Abednego refused to worship the golden image set up by King Nebuchadnezzar (Daniel 3:12) because their foundation was deeply rooted in the wisdom, knowledge, character, and nature of Yahweh. They would not compromise their faith by worshiping a lifeless, manufactured god. To know God and His Word is one thing, but to act upon God's Word and stand on it is something deeper and greater in the eyes of God. The commitment of these Jewish men to following and worshiping the Lord alone reveals a spiritual foundation in their lives that was founded upon God. A shallow spiritual foundation cannot give us a stable devotion and dedication to God or even help us go deeper in the Lord. The deeper things of God call for a deeper foundation because "deep calls to deep" (Psalm 42:7).

If indeed we are desperate for a real revival to sweep through our lives, if we truly desire to live transformed lives, then we need to build deeper and stronger foundations. The world will not believe we are revived and experiencing revival if our lives are not different from theirs. Only good and godly fruit will demonstrate true revival in our lives. Revival is not a one-day experience only but an everyday experience. We must experience God's presence every day in order to continue producing good fruit. Revived people are full of the fruit of the Spirit Paul described in Galatians 5:22–23: love, joy, peace, patience, kindness, goodness, faith, gentleness, and self-control. These character qualities are produced by the Spirit and flow from deep within a believer. If they are not evident in our lives, then we have not yet allowed the Holy Spirit to take total control of our lives. A godly foundation will produce godly fruit that flows from the Spirit of God.

The critical point here is that what is in your heart (foundation) is what you will produce. If you lay a spiritual foundation of peace, you will walk with the spirit of peace; if you lay a foundation of love, you will walk with the spirit of love. You cannot lay a foundation of hatred and expect love to flow from your heart. That is why it is extremely important to lay a foundation based in Jesus Christ. When Christ is the base of your life, you will walk in love and demonstrate a revived life.

What we say, how we treat one another, and what we do reveal to the world whether or not we are indeed sons and daughters of God. Our identity in Christ is proved by how we imitate the character and nature of our Lord Jesus Christ and by the good fruit we produce in our lives. "Yes, the way to identify a tree or a person is by the kind of fruit that is produced" (Matthew 7:20 NLT).

In John 15:8 Jesus said, "My true disciples produce much fruit. This brings great glory to my Father" (NLT). The fruit we produce in our lives is what truly differentiates us from unbelievers and proves to the world that the Spirit of God is actively operating in our lives. If we want God to use us to change the world, we must produce His fruit. God works with faithful, dedicated, passionate, and spiritually fruitful people who have zeal to see Him move in the nations in a mighty way.

STABLE CHRISTIANS INSPIRE PEOPLE FOR GOD

Building a strong spiritual foundation on the foundation of Jesus is the only way we can live a stable spiritual life. Stable Christians will inspire nations and communities to live for God, while unstable Christians will actually cause many people to stumble in their Christian walk because they do not reflect God in their attitudes, actions, and character. When God's people are spiritually stable, strong, and solid in the Lord, no evil forces in this world can stop them from advancing the kingdom of God here on earth. They will influence and change the world as they reflect the character and Spirit of the sovereign God. Immature and unstable Christians get in the way of God's plan for reaching the nations. God's desire is for the church to abandon elementary religious fights and unite in His name to advance His kingdom and help millions of hurting and dying people.

The world is trying to shake and influence the foundation of the body of Christ, but God is calling the body of Christ to rise up and shake the foundation of the world with the power and presence of God. God is calling His people to iron out their differences and unite with one voice, one call, one vision, and one purpose. What is stopping the church from advancing the kingdom of God? It is division within the body of Christ around the world; and this division is due to immaturity and spiritual instability, which in turn is the result of building on faulty foundations.

In 1 John 2:9 John writes, "The one who says he is in the light but hates his brother is in the darkness until now." A person's relationship with other believers is a key indicator of whether he or she is walking in the light or in darkness. God's power operates mightily in an environment where there is unity and love. A good example of this can be seen in the book of Acts. On the day of Pentecost, the believers in Christ "were all with one accord in one place" (Acts 2:1 KJV), when suddenly they experienced the Lord's visitation.

To be in "one accord" simply means to be in agreement, unity, or harmony. Such unity attracts the presence and power of God. No, we cannot agree on every doctrine, but we can all agree that we urgently need the power and presence of God to move like never before in our homes, schools, communities, and nations of the world. The church cannot make the impact it should in the world today unless God's children revisit their spiritual foundation and build a foundation whose base is the Lord Jesus Christ.

The church is not a building; rather, the people of God are the church (1 Corinthians 3:16–17). Consequently, the church is strong and stable only when the people are strong and stable. If the people of God are not spiritually stable but are divided and busy fighting one another, the church will make very little impact here on earth. The Holy Spirit operates powerfully in an environment of love, honor, humility, forgiveness, and peace and not in an environment of pride, hatred, bitterness, unforgiveness, and disunity.

The Holy Spirit works in unity with God the Father and His Son, Jesus Christ. That is why He works powerfully in an environment where unity reigns. Satan, on the other hand, loves working in an environment of disunity, bitterness, and hatred because he is the father of confusion and a deceiver (2 Corinthians 11:3; Revelation 12:9) and he knows the power of unity and a united church.

Through history, we see that God works in unity with His people and through His people to get His work done among the nations. The church is a sleeping giant right now because the people of God are spiritually comfortable in their religion. We need the Spirit of God to revamp our broken spiritual foundations so that the church can be awakened from its slumber. We desperately need a spiritual makeover at both the individual and the corporate level if we are to see God move powerfully in our lives and bring change and transformation to this world.

As God's people, we must stop hiding behind the veil of religion and allow God to do His work in us so that we can be channels through which He changes and touches the world. Being religiously superspiritual on the outside while dysfunctional on the inside will not help us touch the nations of the world. We need the power of God to heal our broken relationships so that we can unite to bring healing to the hurting and freedom to the captives. We must remove the veil of religion from our lives and diligently seek the face of God and allow Him to establish in us a new foundation.

The church has lost its position of influence in the world, and, worse yet, she has lost the glory and power of God. This is because we, the people of God, largely have been building our Christian lives on a defective foundation that cannot house the presence and glory of God. Satan has tampered with the foundation of our lives, and we have compromised our principles. If Jesus were to reveal Himself in power to the church today, it is doubtful we would even recognize Him or accept Him, just as He revealed Himself to the children of Israel centuries ago and they rejected Him because they could not recognize Him as the Messiah sent by God to rescue them (John 1:11).

We need a new foundation because a corrupt foundation (heart) cannot see beyond self. God is looking for a new generation that will look past themselves and stretch out their hands to help the needy, the hurting, and the dying, a generation that will cry out, "The Spirit of the Lord God is upon me, because the Lord has anointed me to bring good news to the poor; he has sent me to bind up the brokenhearted, to proclaim liberty to the captives, and the opening of the prison to those who are bound" (Isaiah 61:1 ESV).

God is looking for a new generation of obedient men and women who will live beyond self. He seeks a generation that does not put self first at the expense of God and His people, a generation that will empower and encourage people to serve the Lord and live for Him sacrificially. God wants a generation that will attract the presence and power of God back to the church.

The world needs a stable church that can make an impact and a difference in the world. Lack of stability in the people of God has caused the body of Christ to lose its position in the world. Spiritual instability also has caused many Christians to be "on and off" in their relationship with God and in the experience of His presence. Today we are strong in the Lord, and tomorrow we are weak; today we believe in God, and tomorrow we doubt His ability and power; today we are on fire for God, and tomorrow we are discouraged and depressed. Spiritually our lives go in the same circle year after year.

We struggle to find balance and stamina in our Christian lives. We attend conference after conference, revival meeting after revival meeting, and deliverance service after deliverance service, and we even change our geographical location; but nothing changes in our lives. We blame our church leaders, our pastor, our friends, and our families for our spiritual struggles and failures, not realizing the main problem is the foundation of our life. When the foundation of our life is ruined, everything becomes unstable and slowly begins to collapse. Indeed, the collapse of families, marriages, moral values, and love for one another that we see in the world is due to broken and faulty spiritual foundations.

Until we deal with things at a foundational level, we will not see the change in our lives we so desire. Addressing the foundational issues of our lives will help us start anew and move us from being dysfunctional to being functional and effective. It also will help prevent our lives from sinking into depression, stress, and sin. Above all, it will help us stop the enemy from overpowering us. The enemy attacks people's life foundation. That foundation is what can give us strength to live for God in a stable way. If Satan manages to break into it and tamper with it, then it becomes very easy for us to live a compromised, defeated Christian life. If, even after much prayer, you are battling the same issues repeatedly in your Christian walk, whether they involve marriage, family, relationships, or anything else, consider the spiritual foundation of your life. The key to victory lies in a strong and deep foundation.

A shallow, weak, and ungodly foundation is one of the root causes of unstable relationships. If you build your foundation with cheap materials, such as the wisdom and knowledge of this world instead of the wisdom and knowledge of God, you will end up struggling most of your Christian life because your foundation is not strong enough to withstand the pressures of life and the evil forces of this world. A robust and well-laid spiritual foundation is your greatest pillar in marriage, business, family, and ministry. The Devil's tactics can never penetrate such a strong spiritual foundation because the anchor of that foundation is the Lord Jesus Christ.

ESCAPISM MENTALITY

Most christians around the world are experiencing a rushing wind of opposition in every dimension of life. This demonic wind has shaken people's foundations and faith in God; it has shaken families, marriages, relationships, and churches. Because of this, many believers in Christ have lost their love, passion, thirst, and desire for the things of God and for God Himself.

Statistics indicate that in North America many shepherds (pastors) are abandoning their sheep (people), and sheep are dropping out of churches in large numbers. Why are these people who loved God, loved worshiping Him, and loved doing His work giving up? There are many factors that are contributing to this, but at the top of the list is the foundational problem. When you lay a shallow foundation in the very beginning, you cannot go very far in life before the forces of this world begin to erode your spiritual life with temptations and ungodly thoughts.

We Christians are finding it increasingly difficult and challenging to faithfully live for God here on earth in an environment that is hostile to the things of God. No doubt that is why many Christians want Jesus Christ to come now and "rapture" them—so that they can escape from this world. But God wants to rule and reign with us here on earth. We are not called to escape from this world but to demonstrate the rule and reign of God. Through us, God wants to demonstrate His mercy, power, and glory to all the world. It is unfortunate that many believers in Christ have built their spiritual lives on the foundation of escapism, constantly looking forward to running away from the troubles of this world instead of demonstrating the power of the almighty God.

The mentality of escapism that has been stirred up by some end-time teachings has caused many people to come to the Lord, not because of love for God but because of fear of going to hell. This has backfired on the church because the world has not yet ended (and only God the Father knows when that day will come), and people are not empowered to live for God here on earth. Instead, they are left struggling to serve God faithfully, not knowing what to do for Him.

We have spiritually weak churches today because of our weak spiritual foundations. The church needs to start afresh and go back to the basics of training God's people properly in the Word of God, helping them establish a new spiritual foundation so that they can function powerfully in today's world. Building our lives on Christ's foundation will empower us to represent the interests of the government of God here on earth in an honorable and powerful way. God's primary interest is to save humanity right now, and His interest must be our interest too. We must not focus on anything but the present interests of the kingdom of God, which are focused on rescuing humankind from the influence and power of Satan.

The mentality, or foundation, of escapism has influenced the minds and hearts of many people for many years till it has reached the point that it now paralyzes the functionality of the church and God's people. It also has weakened and hindered Christians from doing anything for God because their attitude is that the world is "ending very soon." It is not our business to know when the world will end, but it is our business to know and do what God wants to do on the earth through us. We should not let end-time events distract us from doing the present work of God, and we should never build our ministries or Christian lives on these prophesied events. God has provided only one bedrock foundation upon which each one of us must build our lives, and that foundation is Jesus Christ. That means we are here to do what Jesus Christ did when He was here on earth. He preached the good news of the kingdom, and we are to preach the good news of the kingdom; He healed the sick, and we are to heal the sick; and the list goes on.

In John 14:12 Jesus said to His disciples, "The truth is, anyone who believes in me will do the same works I have done, and even greater works, because I am going to be with the Father" (NLT). The task of the disciples of Jesus

Christ was to carry on His ministry and take it even farther. The disciples, working in the power of the Holy Spirit, would carry the good news of God's kingdom from Palestine into the whole world. Our task too is to carry the good news of God's kingdom throughout the whole world. As the Holy Spirit empowers us, we are to do what Jesus did when He walked this earth. Therefore, our duty is to do the works of God, not try to figure out when the world will end.

Chapter 2

If The Foundation Be Destroyed,

What can the righteous do?

> I have taken refuge in the Lord. How can you say to me, "Escape to the mountain like a bird! For look, the wicked string the bow; they put the arrow on the bowstring to shoot from the shadows at the upright in heart. When the foundations are destroyed, what can the righteous do?" (Psalm 11:1–3)

David was advised to run for his life because his enemies were out to get him, but he declared to his advisers that his trust was in the Lord, his refuge. How could they tell him to escape to the mountain like a bird? David's friends were afraid because all they could see were frightening circumstances and crumbling foundations, but David's trust, hope, and faith were in the almighty God. He knew the power and greatness of His God. He knew the enemy could not harm him because the Lord was with him and protecting his life.

Verse 3 asks a very interesting question: "When the foundations are destroyed, what can the righteous do?" David did not give us an explanation or more details about the foundations in view here. Some Bible scholars believe this is a metaphor for something else, and we will look at this closer in our next section on the foundation of law and order. We do not want to read too much into David's statement; however, it is quite significant because it helps us understand the importance of a foundation. Another way of looking at this statement is by asking a counterquestion: What can the righteous *not* do if their foundation is strong, intact, and stable? If the foundation of your life is strong, the Devil cannot prevail against you, and you can do great and mighty things for God.

David's strength was in the Lord. When his enemies were after him, and his friends, with a mentality of escapism, advised him to flee to the mountain, David stood firm and boldly declared, "I have taken refuge in the LORD. How can you say to me, 'Escape to the mountain like a bird!'" Only weak and defenseless people flee from a battle that is not even theirs to fight in the first place. David refused to run because he knew the battle was the Lord's (1 Samuel 17:47), and the Lord was going to rescue him from lawless people. David had made the Lord the foundation of his life.

Birds are defenseless animals. They fly away in panic if disturbed rather than stand their ground and put up a fight. The first thing many people want to do when they are in difficult situations is to fly away in panic like birds to a place of rest and safety (Psalm 55:6). Problems or attacks can tempt us to panic, but in Psalm 11:1 David refused to panic as the wicked aimed their arrows at him, because his foundation was firmly grounded in Yahweh. The best place to run to for rest and safety is into the Lord's presence. We should be running to the presence of God, not running away from His presence. When our foundation is firm and grounded in the Lord, God will be our stability in the midst of troubles. No problem is beyond His ability, no circumstance is too difficult for Him, and no power in the entire universe is able to shake His foundation. If God is not our foundation and we have not built our lives on His Word, we are doomed to destruction. God's people have undermined the foundation of their lives and of the church. That is why the church is struggling today to make a godly impact in the world. Many people today have forsaken God, much like the people in the days of Jeremiah the prophet. God told the Israelites of Jeremiah's day, "My people have done two evil things: They have forsaken me—the fountain of living water. And they have dug for themselves cracked cisterns that can hold no water at all!" (Jeremiah 2:13 NLT).

How can we expect to experience the life and power of God or change the world when we have abandoned God Himself, the fountain of living water and the world changer? The broken cisterns symbolized pagan gods that could not give or sustain life. We too have erected cracked religious foundations and systems that cannot give or sustain life or even hold together our relationship with God or each other. We need to return to God, our foundation, if we are to make an impact in this world for His kingdom. The most dangerous thing we can ever do is build our lives on a cracked religious foundation or on man's doctrines and traditions. Here is King Solomon's warning: "Unless the Lord builds a house, its builders labor over it in vain; unless the Lord watches over a city, the watchman stays alert in vain" (Psalm 127:1).

The theme of this wisdom psalm (Psalm 127) is that without the Lord's favor and protection, our labor is worthless. There is no way we can do the work of God or advance His kingdom without His presence and power. God alone is the source of strength, shelter, life, refuge, and power. On our own, we are nothing and subject to defeat; but if we build our lives on God's foundation, no power in this world is able to bring us down.

The strength of a Christian is found in God's strength, and God's strength is deeply rooted in His righteousness and justice. Psalm 89:14 declares, "Righteousness and justice are the foundation of Your throne; faithful love and truth go before You." Righteousness and justice serve as the base or platform upon which God builds His majesty. Righteousness, justice, faithful love, and truth summarize God's powerful attributes and character. Because He is righteous, faithful, and truthful and He loves justice, He will defend us, protect us, and watch over us. We do not have to flee like a bird when we are in trouble but can stand firm on His Word. Where our strength cannot take us, God's strength can. We must faithfully depend on God and not trust, or depend on, our own wisdom or ability.

THE FOUNDATION OF LAW AND ORDER

Let us explore Psalm 11:3 a little deeper now: "When the foundations are destroyed, what can the righteous do?" David does not state or describe to us exactly what these foundations are, but most Bible scholars believe he may have been referring to moral foundations, or the principles of justice within society. To support this view, the New Living Translation translates Psalm 11:3: "The foundations of law and order have collapsed. What can the righteous do?"

If indeed the reference is to the moral foundations of law and order, or the principles of justice within society, then it is worthwhile for us to look at the meaning of the word *law.* It is especially important to look at law from a Hebrew perspective because most of us view the "law" as stiff regulations. Because of a Greek and Western mind-set, we have come to view God's instructions such as the Ten Commandments in a similar manner. This has led many Christians to throw away the Ten Commandments, insisting that Jesus abolished the law and appealing (out of context) to Romans 10:4.

The word *law* in Greek is *nomos;* the equivalent in Hebrew is *torah.* The word *torah* literally means teaching or instruction; so the "law of God" is simply God's teaching or instruction that gives us insight into all aspects of life so that we may know how to conduct ourselves, how to treat one another, how to approach God, and how to live with each other. The *torah,* or the law, always points to the Messiah. We fall into error, however, if we try to make the law a means for achieving our own righteousness or salvation. The law is there to show us how far short of God's standards we fall. We receive righteousness through faith in Jesus Christ our Savior. Christ, the sinless Son of God, took our sins upon Himself and became the willing, perfect sacrifice, suffering the punishment we deserved.

The law of God is not there to get us into trouble but to get us out of trouble and to show the nations and the community the ways of God. God's instruction or teaching is what gives us the guidance we need to represent Him and His kingdom here on earth. When God's instructions are undermined in our lives or cast aside, the result is mayhem in the community and in the nations of the world. The Word of God is what holds together the foundation of law and order in the world and in the body of Christ. That is why most governments use the Bible to swear people into office, and in most courts of law witnesses swear on the Bible to affirm they are telling nothing but the truth. The Word of God is the anchor of unity, life, and peace. Without knowing and doing the Word of God, it is impossible to live in peace with each other.

From what we can tell, David's enemies had no respect for God's teaching or guidance on how to live with each other in society, which is why they had the courage to pursue David and attempt to kill him. In other words, the foundation of the Lord's teaching or instruction in the hearts of David's enemies had collapsed; so killing was a normal thing for them to do. The actions of the wicked, or lawless, in the community shake the foundations of law and order and justice and morality. In addition, they drastically alter or destroy the order of living established by God, which centers on loving God with all of our heart and loving our neighbor as ourselves (human respect).

> They do not know or understand; they wander in darkness.
> All the foundations of the earth are shaken. (Psalm 82:5)

When the foundation of morality and justice within society or within the body of Christ is tampered with, the result is immorality and injustice. For example, look at Syria today. How can a nation that respects and values God's teaching on human life and dignity use chemical weapons on innocent children, women, and men? The use of chemical weapons by Syria on its own people has shaken the foundations of international law and order because it has shaken the foundations of the moral principles God instilled in the creation order.

Upholding the foundation of the Lord's teaching (law) on how to live for Him and how to treat and live with each other is very important to us because God's teaching is the blueprint for living a peaceful and joyful life. The problem the church is facing today is due to the collapse of the foundation of God's teaching in the body of Christ and in believers' hearts. We live as though we are not children of the living God at all. We need to go back to the Word of God and reestablish it as the governing authority of our lives and of the church.

We are struggling in our lives, relationships, families, and marriages simply because we have neglected the Word of God. Many preachers around the world are busy teaching people how to get wealthy but are neglecting the Word of God and the spiritual well-being of God's people. What we need is not prosperity but God's presence, and we need a revival of knowing and obeying the Word of God.

God knows that a world without the foundation of law and order will be a world filled with calamity for His creatures, both physically and spiritually. Therefore, He gave us pillars, or foundations, to serve as anchors of our relationship with Him and with each other. These foundations are called the Ten Commandments. When God gave the Ten Commandments through Moses to the Jewish people, He was giving them the foundation of law and order for their physical and spiritual well-being. Today God has given us a greater, stronger, and firmer pillar to hold our lives together: His Son Jesus Christ.

God is a foundation builder. Before establishing or building anything tangible or new, He lays a foundation in place. We see this in the book of Exodus. God delivered the Israelites from the slavery and brutality of Pharaoh, and His plan was to build them into a strong community of believers who would worship, honor, and reverence His name without compromise. In order for God to make the Israelites a strong nation and a light to the world, the Israelites needed a fresh start and a strong foundation in place.

It is impossible to serve God effectively without having and following His commands and guidance. One interesting thing about a foundation is that it gives the builder guidance on how to build according to the architect's design or style. In Exodus 20 God gave Moses the Ten Commandments as a foundation upon which the Israelites could build their spiritual life and relationship with God according to His designed plan.

It is also very important to understand that God gave the Ten Commandments to humankind as a foundation, or pillar, of law and order upon which the community of believers could base their day-to-day lives for the benefit of the entire community and the kingdom of God. The Ten Commandments are not legalistic rules; rather, they act as a sharpening stone that sharpens and shapes our faith and trust in God. The law of God is good and beneficial. Psalm 119 helps us see the goodness of the law of God and the benefits it brings into our lives.

- The law of God brings order and direction into our lives: "I pondered the direction of my life, and I turned to follow your statutes" (Psalm 119:59 NLT).
- The commandments of God bring life: "I will never forget your commandments, for by them you give me life" (Psalm 119:93).
- God's commandments can make us wiser and give us steady and stable guidance in our lives: "Your commands make me wiser than my enemies, for they are my constant guide" (Psalm 119:98).

God gave the Ten Commandments to the Jewish people for their physical, social, and spiritual well-being. Understanding these foundations will help us live a godly life that demonstrates the characteristics of God in us. If Christ is living in us, then it should be impossible for us to willingly worship idols, misuse His name, commit adultery, murder, steal, and give a false testimony against someone.

For our *spiritual well-being,* God gave the following commandments to His people:

- "You shall have no other gods before me." (Exodus 20:3; Deuteronomy 5:7 ESV)
- "You shall not make for yourself a carved image." (Exodus 20:4; Deuteronomy 5:8 ESV)
- "Do not misuse the name of the LORD your God." (Exodus 20:7; Deuteronomy 5:11 NLT)
- "Observe the Sabbath day by keeping it holy." (Exodus 20:8; Deuteronomy 5:12 NLT)

These first four commandments were given as foundations upon which the children of God were to build their relationship with Yahweh. For the well-being of the Jewish people and the maintenance of a strong relationship with Yahweh, the Jews had to avoid worshiping idols and misusing the Lord's name. In addition, in order for them to stay close to the Lord and show their commitment to Him, they had to stand on these four commandments. Doing otherwise would cause them to stray easily from God's presence and act wickedly. Without walking under the authority and leadership of the Holy Spirit and the Word of God, it is always easy to stray from the presence of God.

Many Christians are giving up on serving God and living for Him. Many of us are not walking under the authority and leadership of the Holy Spirit and the Word of God. We all, like sheep, have gone astray; each of us has turned to his or her own ways because the fear of God has disappeared from our hearts. Jesus Christ paid for our sins so that we can draw close to God the Father and walk under the authority and leadership of His Spirit. We need to rebuild the foundation of honor and respect for the Lord in our lives if we are to see the power of God fully manifested. Often, it seems we have become just too "familiar" with God, and that is why we are prone to straying from His presence. Let us maintain honor and respect for God both individually and corporately. God is worthy of honor, He is worthy of worship, and He is worthy of our praise; let us lift His name up, for there is no name above His.

For our *social well-being,* and the well-being of humanity as a whole, God gave the following commandments:

- "Honor your father and your mother so that you may have a long life in the land that the Lord your God is giving you." (Exodus 20:12; cf. Deuteronomy 5:16)
- "Do not murder." (Exodus 20:13; Deuteronomy 5:17)
- "Do not commit adultery." (Exodus 20:14; Deuteronomy 5:18)
- "Do not steal." (Exodus 20:15; Deuteronomy 5:19)
- "Do not give false testimony against your neighbor." (Exodus 20:16; cf. Deuteronomy 5:20)
- "Do not covet . . . anything that belongs to your neighbor." (Exodus 20:17; Deuteronomy 5:21)

The last six commandments are for the well-being of people in a community. For the people of God to enjoy God's provision of long life, they needed to honor their fathers and mothers. In addition, for them to respect the dignity of another person, which involved that person's life and family, God required them not to commit murder, adultery, or theft, or give false testimony against someone, or covet what belonged to another. These decrees gave structure to God's people and distinguished them from lawless and pagan people of their generation. Today the world has adopted many of God's teachings in order to maintain law and order in the nations. We all know what happens to a person who steals somebody's property, commits murder, or falsely testifies against an innocent person in a court of law. The instructions (law) of the Lord are good and not burdensome. In fact, we who have the Lord Jesus Christ (who is the goal of the law) living inside of us should easily be able to obey the Word of God and live a lifestyle that demonstrates the character of Jesus Christ.

A country or a world without the foundation of law and order will see great damage done to society, to human life, and above all to the dignity of God the Creator. God is a God of order; He created everything perfect at an appointed time and according to His supernatural plan and design. Nothing He created or gave to His creation was accidental or by mistake. His law was not given to His children by mistake. We can argue various points of theology, but only the Word of God will stand forever. What is important is for us to hear, know, and do the Word of God and allow it to transform our lives.

Yes, Jesus is the fulfillment and the goal of the law, but that does not mean we should ignore God's teaching on how to live in harmony with Him and with one another. The foundation of God's law and order is critical to the stability of the world and to our spiritual lives. People who kill other human beings—even in the name of God—or steal another person's property have not yet experienced the true, living God.

The law (teaching) of God is the spiritual foundation of our lives. His Word is a lamp to guide our feet and a light for our path (Psalm 119:105). However, if this foundation of our life is undermined, what can we, the righteous of Christ, do? We can easily become vulnerable to Satan's attacks and influence and stray from the presence of God.

One reason many people in the world are becoming lovers of self, lovers of money, boastful, proud, abusive, disobedient to parents, ungrateful, irreconcilable, slanderers, without self-control, brutal, without love for what is good, treacherous, conceited, and lovers of pleasure rather than lovers of God (2 Timothy 3:1–4) is because of the faulty foundation of their lives. It is unfortunate that even Christians are being consumed by the influence of the world and thus have undermined the foundation of God's teaching for their lives.

Satan aims his arrows at the hearts of believers in Christ because in the heart is the foundation of strength, purpose, persistence, and determination. To hold on to the Word of God in our heart is to stand on God's solid foundation. We must build our life, not according to the traditions of man, but according to God's plan and design. We are strong and powerful, not because of man, but because of the Lord Jesus Christ and His Word.

In 2 Timothy 3:13–15 Paul advised Timothy,

> Evil people and impostors will become worse, deceiving and being deceived. But as for you, continue in what you have learned and firmly believed. You know those who taught you, and you know that from childhood you have known the sacred Scriptures, which are able to give you wisdom for salvation through faith in Christ Jesus.

The Word of God has the power to keep us focused on God despite Satan's attempts to deceive us and turn us away from God through useless disputes and ungodliness. We must never let the Word of God depart from our hearts because God watches over His Word to perform it (Jeremiah 1:12).

In Deuteronomy 11:16–19, God gave this instruction to His people:

> But do not let your heart turn away from the LORD to worship other gods. If you do, the Lord's anger will burn

> against you. He will shut up the sky and hold back the rain, and your harvests will fail. Then you will quickly die in that good land the LORD is now giving you. So commit yourselves completely to these words of mine. Tie them to your hands as a reminder, and wear them on your forehead. Teach them to your children. Talk about them when you are at home and when you are away on a journey, when you are lying down and when you are getting up again. (NLT)

Here God is warning His covenant people not to turn from Him to worship and bow down to Baal, Asherah, Astarte, and other gods and goddesses who were thought to generate and sustain life. He reminds His people of the importance of remaining faithful to Him and to His Word, and He encourages them to pass along His instructions to their children so that their days and those of their children may be many in the land He swore to give to their ancestors.

Proverbs 3:1–4 also encourages us not to forget God's teaching:

> My son, don't forget my teaching, but let your heart keep my commands; for they will bring you many days, a full life, and well-being. Never let loyalty and faithfulness leave you. Tie them around your neck; write them on the tablet of your heart. Then you will find favor and high regard in the sight of God and man.

As we continue our study, we will look further at the importance of the heart and look even deeper at the power of the Word of God. The body of Christ has reached a point where everyone does what is pleasing in his or her own eyes. This is because we have built our lives on a faulty foundation and on teachings that do not center on the Word of God or on Christ.

Upon hearing that there was serious dissension among the churches of Galatia, Paul wrote in Galatians 5:15, "But if you bite and devour one another, watch out, or you will be consumed by one another." We are biting and devouring one another by way of gossip and character assassination.

We are busy competing with each other at the expense of the broken-hearted and dying. We are focused on ourselves instead of on the plans and will of God for this hour. There is no unity in the church or in the world today because the foundation of unity has collapsed. There is no honor and respect for God or for His servants because the foundation of honor and respect has collapsed. There is no honor and respect for each other or for parents because the foundation of honor and respect for parents has collapsed. And there is no "fear of God" (awe, reverence) in the church today because the foundation of the fear of God in our lives has collapsed.

It is clear the enemy has tampered with our spiritual foundation, and the only way to reverse this is by rebuilding that spiritual foundation according to God's design and not according to man's design. We are what we are and where we are today because of the foundation of our lives. We have changed outwardly, but inwardly we are still the same. Consequently, we are still struggling, empty, and broken. May God revive our hearts and transform our lives so that we can manifest His glory and power. The world is tired of a powerless and empty religion.

CHAPTER 3

The Heart

(THE ENGINE OF OUR SPIRITUAL LIFE)

The human heart is the most influential part of our spiritual life. Indeed, it is the engine of our spiritual life. "In Biblical language, [the heart is] the center of the human spirit, from which spring emotions, courage and action."[2] It is in the heart that we establish either a strong and deep foundation or a weak and shallow one. Since the heart is the center of our spiritual life, the place where our foundation is erected, it is essentially equivalent to a person's spiritual foundation. It is no surprise, then, that Satan's primary goal is to attack a person's heart and destroy his or her spiritual foundation.

Protecting the heart against evil thoughts or false ideas is one of the most important duties of a Christian. The heart not only is the base or source of our intentions, emotions, trust, and life but also is the center of our relationship with God and with each other. Any successful assault on our heart will affect our whole being.

In Proverbs 4:23 King Solomon said, "Above all else, guard your heart, for it affects everything you do" (NLT). If your heart is strong in the Lord, pure and determined to serve Him regardless of your situation in life, no weapon can shake who you are in Christ or destroy you. However, if your heart is full of fear, wrong motives, selfish ambition, hatred, strife, and

---

2 *NIV Study Bible* (Grand Rapids: Zondervan, 2002), 791, note on Psalm 4:7.

unforgiveness, the Devil will prevail against you, because he thrives in such environments.

> The human heart is most deceitful and desperately wicked. Who really knows how bad it is? But I know! I, the LORD, search all hearts and examine secret motives. I give all people their due rewards, according to what their actions deserve. (Jeremiah 17:9–10 NLT)

In Jeremiah 17:9–10 we see that the battle is in the heart. When God examines our lives, He does not look at our outward spirituality or our mind; He looks at the heart, the engine of our being and actions. In other words, God is interested greatly in our hearts. If His Spirit can capture and take hold of our hearts, we will be the people of His pasture and the sheep under His care. Jeremiah reminds us of the wickedness of the heart so that we can do something about it; namely, guard it. Sometimes we forget how bad the heart can be because we concentrate too much on the mind. Nevertheless, God examines the heart and not the mind because the heart is the source of everything we say and do in relation to God and each other.

> Guard your heart above all else, for it is the source of life. (Proverbs 4:23)

To guard something simply means to make sure it does not get away and that it is safe from any attacks. In Hebrew thought, the heart is the location of knowledge and the preconscious source of decisions. The condition of one's heart indicates one's true character. The heart is the engine of our faith in God; if it is not protected against the influence of the world, our life in God is adversely affected. Faith in God is developed and maintained in the heart, not in the mind. When Scripture says, "Guard your heart above all else," that means we must pay attention to what goes into it. No one guards what is worthless but only what is valuable. The heart is extremely valuable, not only in a physical or natural sense, but also in a spiritual sense, because it is the essence of who we are and the core of our being.

The heart is a pillar of our spiritual life, and thus it is under constant attack. Satan uses all kinds of weapons to attack the heart. He uses disappointment, false accusations, discouragement, and negative words and thoughts to try to derail a person's heart from focusing on the greatness and goodness of God. It is vital to establish a strong foundation in the Word of God in your heart, a foundation that is centered on biblical principles, not on worldly principles or views. You can be sure Satan will test the strength of your spiritual foundation repeatedly; so build a solid foundation so that you do not fall into his traps.

The true test of our spiritual foundation will come by way of the storms of life. Some things we go through in our lives, or may currently be going through, can either break us down or build us up. With a strong foundation, we can weather any storms in our lives and even use those storms to build ourselves up in our faith. A strong and successful Christian life is determined by the strength of the heart. With a strong heart, we can go all the way for the kingdom of God; but with a faint, weak heart, we can easily be crushed by the storms of life and give up on God.

Take good care of your heart. Nurture it with the Word of God. Don't allow unnecessary pressure or negative words to take up residence in your heart. Make the Holy Spirit the only resident of your heart, because whatever is in your heart your mouth will speak. Have you ever been around a person who made an inappropriate statement and then quickly retracted it, saying, "Sorry; it was a slip of the tongue"? It wasn't a slip of a tongue; it was the manifestation of the person's heart. Whatever we speak or do flows from the content of the heart. If the heart is not changed and transformed by the power of the Holy Spirit, it is impossible to change what we do or say. Change begins by feeding the mind and heart with the Word of God on a daily basis and applying it in our lives. The heart, not the head, determines how deeply we are connected to God. The depth of our connection to God and to His Spirit is demonstrated by the character and nature of our lives.

YOUR HEART REFLECTS YOU

Proverbs 27:19 says, "As the water reflects the face, so the heart reflects the person." The ESV translation puts it this way: "As in water face reflects face, so the heart of man reflects the man." Your heart is who you are, the real you and the source of everything you do and become. What you do and say comes from your heart. We trust God, not in the mind but in the heart. It is in our heart where Jesus Christ becomes our foundation. His character, mercy, love, power, life, and deeds become the center of our life. That means we love as He loves, we forgive as He forgives, and we see the world and people as He sees them.

> "You brood of snakes! How could evil men like you speak what is good and right? For whatever is in your heart determines what you say. A good person produces good words from a good heart, and an evil person produces evil words from an evil heart." (Matthew 12:34–35 NLT)

Here Jesus was speaking to the Pharisees of His day. The evil words spoken by the Pharisees revealed the true nature of their hearts. The Pharisees considered themselves righteous, but their actions, attitudes, and character did not live up to that standard. Jesus told them that whatever is in a person's heart determines what the person says. A good person produces good things from the treasury of a good heart, and an evil person produces evil things from the treasury of an evil heart. What comes out of one's mouth reveals what is in that person's heart. We can know if Jesus Christ is a person's "foundation" by the words that come out of the person's mouth and by that person's actions, character, and attitude. Likewise, we can know our own foundation by looking at our words, actions, attitudes, and character. Does our character demonstrate the life of Christ in us? If not, we need to revisit our spiritual foundation.

God searches the heart of a person; He does not look merely at the outward appearance. God judges us by faith and character and not by appearance (1 Samuel 16:7). God is and always has been after His people's hearts because our hearts are at the very core of our lives. Satan also targets the human heart. He fights to corrupt and influence it because if God's people have pure hearts, the kingdom of darkness has no power or influence over their lives. This is why the heart must be protected from all evil at all times. What we allow to influence our heart is going to dominate our life and determine what we become. It is in the heart where we establish the Lord Jesus Christ as our bedrock. Our lives must completely depend on Christ for wisdom, knowledge, direction, peace, strength, and life.

Jesus is after our hearts because our hearts *determine* our true spiritual condition. They also *reveal* our spiritual condition. No one can hide his or her heart from the eyes of God. We can hide from each other but not from God. People often try to hide corrupt hearts behind the façade of religion, even as they did in Jesus' day. But Jesus said of such persons, "These people honor me with their lips, but their hearts are far away. Their worship is a farce, for they replace God's commands with their own man-made teachings" (Matthew 15:8–9 NLT).

Jesus was quoting the words of Isaiah the prophet, who also criticized half-hearted people in his day (Isaiah 29:13). In particular, Jesus was criticizing the religious leaders. They knew a lot about God, but their hearts had nothing to show for it and were far away from Him. Religion for theses religious leaders had become routine; it was not real. They claimed to be close to God, but they were hypocrites who merely went through the motions. As they say, actions speak louder than words, and these religious leaders' actions and attitudes loudly declared that their hearts were far from God.

A transformed heart will demonstrate the goodness of God and illustrate His character for all to see God's work and power in you. What you do, what you say, and how you say it mirrors what is in your heart, which is the root of your foundation. You cannot say, do, or give anything but what is in your heart. The only way to change what is in you is by changing what is in your heart at the very foundation of your belief system, emotions, and thoughts. You cannot say you have changed if your heart is still demonstrating the past things of your life.

TRANSFORMATION

When we accept the rule and reign of Christ and His influence upon our lives, the transformation begins in our hearts. This does not mean we become "perfect," but it certainly should cause us to live differently than before and in the light of Jesus Christ, our righteousness. If there is no evidence of change in our lives, then we must check the depth of our spiritual foundation.

The depth of your spiritual foundation in the Lord and in the Word of God will determine the level of transformation in your life. Your spiritual foundation is only as deep as your devotion to and understanding of God's Word. The deeper you are in the Word of God, the deeper and stronger your spiritual foundation will be; and the shallower you are in the Word of God, the shallower and weaker your spiritual foundation will be.

As we draw near to God and to His presence, we go deeper in Him, and God begins to change our very identity and life, allowing us to serve and live for Him effectively. James writes, "Draw near to God, and He will draw near to you. Cleanse your hands, sinners, and purify your hearts, double-minded people!" (James 4:8). James was addressing the issue that causes fighting and disputes among God's people: pride. However, as we draw near to God, God draws near to us; and transformation begins to take place as we allow His Spirit to cleanse and purify our hearts. With the help of the Holy Spirit, we can put off our old, prideful self, which belongs to our former manner of life.

Romans 6 describes our transformation as uniting with Jesus Christ both in His death and in His resurrection. In Christ, we are dead to our former lifestyle and resurrected into newness of life in Him. Our evil desires and bondage to sin died with Christ because we are united with Him by faith. We are restored to live a lifestyle that reflects the culture of the kingdom of God and not the culture of this world. The sinful foundation Adam laid for us has been broken, and sin has no hold on us. Jesus has laid a new foundation for us, a foundation of righteousness. The power of sin over us died with Christ on the cross, and we are free from its power.

Transformation is a process that takes time, as we build upon our foundation in Christ. It is not something we can achieve overnight. It requires discipline, dedication, and a passion for God. The past may try to rise up in our life, but we must determine to stay close to the presence of God. As we stay in the Word and in God's presence, transformation begins to take place in our lives.

We all, with unveiled faces, are looking as in a mirror at the glory of the Lord and are being transformed into the same image from glory to glory; this is from the Lord who is the Spirit. (2 Corinthians 3:18)

God's desire and plan for us as believers in Christ is to transform us from one level of glory in Him to another. The veil of our past lifestyle, which keeps us from moving forward in the Lord, must be cut off from our lives. As we gaze at the nature of God with unveiled minds and hearts, we become more like our Lord Jesus Christ and move from glory to glory. Becoming Christlike is a progressive work that is accomplished by the Holy Spirit. The Holy Spirit is the one who works in us to change us into vessels of God. All we need to do is allow Him to work in us and desire for Him to change us so that we can be powerful ambassadors of the kingdom of God here on earth. It is a wise thing to open our lives up to God and humbly ask Him to help us deal with our weaknesses. We all have weaknesses; and if those weaknesses are not dealt with, they can lead us away from the presence of God.

We should never be ashamed to honestly go before God and ask Him to change some things in our lives. God knows us better than anyone else knows us, and we can never hide from Him anyway. It is important to understand that we are called to live for God and please Him, not to please man. What keeps many of us from experiencing real transformation is our man-pleasing spirit. We put on a spiritual show only to be seen by others and to look good before them, instead of living to give God honor and glory. When we cast away the spirit of pleasing man and begin to please God in all we do, we will attract many to the kingdom of God.

A NEW HEART AND A RIGHT SPIRIT

King David understood the importance of having a pure and clean heart before God. After he had sinned before God, he cried out to Him in Psalm 51:10, "Create in me a clean heart and renew a right spirit within me." The word *create* here simply means to bring something new into existence that is not already there, something that cannot emerge from what now is and that only God can create or design. After Nathan the prophet had confronted David over his sin (2 Samuel 12:7–14), David realized the spiritual condition of his heart was far from being pure before God and his spirit wasn't right either; so he humbled himself before God and cried out to Him to create in him a new heart and to renew a right spirit within him.

When the Spirit of God creates in us a "new heart" and "a right spirit" and the old and corrupt spirit, or nature, and its influence are washed away, He fills us with godly desires. A new "heart" symbolizes a new beginning and a transformed life. A right spirit comes from a new heart; and a new and transformed heart allows us to live for God honorably. For David to correct and change his character, he needed a new heart and a clean spirit. In the body of Christ today, we need renewed hearts and right spirits if we are to demonstrate the kingdom of heaven here on earth.

The content and state of our heart produces our actions and behavior. Out of the abundance of our heart, our mouth speaks. If we fill our heart with the Spirit of God, we will produce the fruit of the Spirit. If we fill our heart with bitterness, our actions will be in accordance with the bitterness that is in us. God is interested in the human heart because it is the center of our spiritual life.

We can never please God with outward actions if our hearts are far from Him. God desires a broken spirit and heart above acts of sacrifice (Psalm 51:16–17). He is near those who are broken and humble (Psalm 34:18). He rejects those who have hearts of stone (Ezekiel 11:19; 36:26) and resists the proud, but He gives grace to the humble (James 4:6).

In Ezekiel 36:26–28 God made a promise to His people:

> I will give you a new heart and put a new spirit within you; I will remove your heart of stone and give you a heart of flesh. I will place My Spirit within you and cause you to follow my statutes and carefully observe my ordinances. Then you will live in the land that I gave your fathers; you will be my people, and I will be your God.

We see the same promise in the book of Deuteronomy: "The Lord your God will circumcise your heart and the hearts of your descendants, and you will love Him with all your heart and all your soul so that you will live" (Deuteronomy 30:6).

These scriptures show us how important our heart is to God. God desires to transform the heart above all else because life flows from the heart. God promised to restore Israel not only physically but also spiritually. To accomplish this, God would give them a new heart and put His Spirit within them. In giving them a new heart, He would be giving them a "new foundation" of life, which would allow them to live for Him. Their old heart, or "old foundation," would not allow them to follow God. It was corrupted by the spirit of pagan idol worship. To build a new foundation is to establish a new base in the heart. And what comes out of the new heart is different from what came out of the old heart that preceded it. That is why Paul says in 2 Corinthians 5:17, "If anyone is in Christ, he is a new creation; old things have passed away, and new things have come."

When we surrender our heart to Jesus Christ, He gives us a new heart and takes away the heart of stone so that we can live a different life, a life that reflects the kingdom of God rather than the kingdom of this world. If you are born again and your life is not reflecting a lifestyle consistent with the kingdom of God, there is something wrong at a foundational level. In Christ, we have been given a new identity and nature, an identity and nature very different from what previously characterized us. Through Christ, we are able to live a victorious life. He alone is a tried and tested foundation upon which we can build our lives safely and securely. No foundation is stronger, more secure, or more worthy of trust than that of our Lord Jesus Christ. In Him we can live out our Christian lives with power and confidence.

CHAPTER 4

A Tried and Tested Foundation: Jesus

> Therefore the Lord God said: "Look, I have laid a stone in Zion, a tested stone, a precious cornerstone, a sure foundation; the one who believes will be unshakable." (Isaiah 28:16)

The NLT translates Isaiah 28:16, "Therefore, this is what the Sovereign LORD says: 'Look! I am placing a foundation stone in Jerusalem. It is firm, a tested and precious cornerstone that is safe to build on. Whoever believes need never run away again.'"

Isaiah here is speaking of a foundation stone, a precious cornerstone God was going to establish in Zion. It would be a foundation that was firm and tested, and that foundation would be the Messiah, Jesus Christ. Jesus is not only a tried and tested foundation upon which we all should build our lives, but He is also a trustworthy foundation. In the wilderness Satan tested and tried Jesus with temptations, but Jesus overcame the Devil and his temptations (Matthew 4:1–11).

When Adam and Eve were tempted by Satan in the garden of Eden, they failed miserably; but Jesus Christ overcame the Devil. He defeated the power of sin and death, and by so doing He established a base upon which we can confidently and safely build our lives. To build our lives on Him is to build on a tried and tested foundation that cannot be shaken or moved.

Jesus Christ also is a living cornerstone, and when we build our lives on His foundation, we become alive in Him.

IN CHRIST WE ARE LIVING STONES

> Come to Christ, who is the living cornerstone of God's temple. He was rejected by the people, but he is precious to God who chose him. And now God is building you, as living stones, into his spiritual temple. What's more, you are God's holy priests, who offer the spiritual sacrifices that please him because of Jesus Christ. As the Scriptures express it, "I am placing a stone in Jerusalem, a chosen cornerstone, and anyone who believes in him will never be disappointed." (1 Peter 2:4–6 NLT)

Colossians 1:17 says of Jesus, "He is before all things, and by Him all things hold together." Jesus Christ, the visible image of the invisible God, is a sure foundation. In Him, our lives are held together, kept safe from harm, and prevented from falling apart. He is the upholder of all life; no Christian can stand in this world without standing in the strength and power of Jesus. He alone is the anchor of life, the living cornerstone of God's temple, and we believers are living stones built into a spiritual house. Christ is the foundation and cornerstone of the church; and because He is a life-giving cornerstone, all believers have been given new life and made His holy priests. We believers together are a "spiritual house." One stone is not a spiritual house or a temple, and one body part is useless without other body parts. Each body part needs other body parts in order for the whole body to function properly; likewise, as the body of Christ, we need each other.

As a chosen people, a royal priesthood, a holy nation, and God's very own possession (1 Peter 2:9), we need to establish a strong foundation so that we can proclaim the praises of the One who has called us out of darkness and demonstrate to the world the goodness of His kingdom. When we build our lives on the foundation of Christ, we are building on a foundation that can never be destroyed or shaken. No flood, no strong wind, no tsunami, no hurricane, and no other power on earth is able to shake Jesus Christ, the foundation, and neither can any power shake the lives of those who build on Him.

Many believers today have made the mistake of building their spiritual lives on the foundation of this world: money, pride, pleasure, self-seeking, the doctrines and traditions of man, or worldly wisdom. As a result of this, the church is experiencing what we might call a spiritual recession. A life built on the foundation of the spirit of this world has no power to sustain or change lives. If we are to be world changers, we need to build our lives on the foundation of the character and nature of God. We are not making an impact in the world today because nearly everything seems to center on us and not on God. We put money, material things, and ourselves before God. Our emphasis is on what God can give to us and not on what we can give to Him or do for the kingdom of God. The apostle Paul foresaw such a time when he wrote to Timothy.

> For people will love only themselves and their money. They will be boastful and proud, scoffing at God, disobedient to their parents, and ungrateful. They will consider nothing sacred. They will be unloving and unforgiving; they will slander others and have no self-control; they will be cruel and have no interest in what is good. (2 Timothy 3:2–3 NLT)

We cannot change the entire corrupt religious system that is so prevalent in the world today, but we can surely protect ourselves from its corruption and effect upon our lives by living according to the Word of God and not according to the traditions or doctrines of man. We can desire to be a different kind of Christian, shining with the light of God and inspiring others to look to the Light of the World: Jesus Christ. We cannot control how others live for God, but we can control how we live for Him. We are each responsible for how we live for God; so let us never blame anyone for our weak and unstable relationship with God or for our failure to stay on fire for Him. Our spiritual life should never depend on what man does or does not do but on God alone. God has given us His Son Jesus Christ as the bedrock of our faith, hope, and life. Because of Christ in us, we have the power to resist the influence of the world and forcefully advance His kingdom. We are living stones, not dead stones; and the function of each living stone is to give life, strength, and stability to the body of Christ. God's people are set apart to minister life to the lifeless and hope to the hopeless.

In 2 Corinthians 6:17 Paul says, "Therefore come out from them and be separate, says the Lord. Touch no unclean thing, and I will receive you" (NIV). Separation from a corrupt religious world or system involves more than just keeping our distance from its influence; it means getting closer to God and letting Him influence us in all that we do or desire to do. That means Jesus Christ must take the center stage of our life and rule and reign in us. We are called to pull away from the things that do not help us grow or mature in the Lord. Anything that does not motivate us to live for God is not worth holding on to; we must let it go. There are many things we hold on to in our lives that are not beneficial to our spiritual well-being. Through the power of God, we can free ourselves from those things that hold us back from pursuing God wholeheartedly.

In 2 Peter 3:17 Peter cautioned believers to be on their guard so that they are not led away by the error of lawless people and thus fall from their stable position. He also encouraged them to grow in the grace and knowledge of Jesus Christ. To continue in the Lord, serving Him faithfully and steadfastly, we need to guard our lives against things that may pull us away from God. There is no other strong foundation upon which we can build our life, ministry, and marriage apart from Jesus Christ, our foundation. In the next chapter, we are going to look at how we can build a strong spiritual foundation in our lives, a foundation that is unshakable and built on the foundation of Christ and His nature.

The strength of your Christianity will not be measured by how many times you go to church but by how you withstand the storms of life. If Jesus Christ is your true foundation, you will be able to stand faithfully in Him during the most difficult times of your life. In life you will go through difficult and devastating times. Will you have the stamina, endurance, tenacity, and perseverance to continue standing and moving forward without losing your faith in God and your love for Him? Most Christians seem to give up on God when the floods and storms of life hit them hard, and they begin questioning the goodness and even the existence of God.

God is still God in the flood or storm, in the sun or rain, and in good times or bad times. He never changes or slumbers; He watches over His people day and night. A strong foundation in life will equip you to stand strong in the Lord even when things around you are falling apart. You are only as strong as the depth of your life foundation. If your foundation is weak, everything in your life will be unstable. You can get "revived" today by the presence of God but after a few days be spiritually weak again. A strong spiritual foundation not only will make your Christian life stable but also will sustain your life and faith in God.

Chapter 5

Building A Strong Foundation

Laying a strong spiritual foundation is not a simple thing to do or something one rushes through; it requires time, planning, and suitable materials. The strength and stability of a building is dependent on the quality of its foundation. A building may look attractive on the outside, but the strength of its foundation is the most important thing to look at, not its outward attractiveness. Likewise, Christians may be zealous, devoted to church, have a good knowledge of God's Word, and speak the Christian "language" but still be weak in faith and unstable in their relationship with God. What is important is not *just* our zeal for and knowledge of God's Word—though those are important—but a personal relationship with God. When we have a strong personal relationship with God, our zeal, strength, and passion for God will be dynamic. The foundation of our relationship and fellowship with God is very important. A strong and stable biblical foundation is key to having a strong and stable relationship and fellowship with God.

God does not look at the outward appearance as we do. When Samuel was looking for a king to anoint, God advised him not to judge by the appearance or height because He does not judge people based on their outward appearance. Rather, He looks at the heart, which is the source of faith and character (1 Samuel 16:7). Similarly, some Christians may look strong, spiritual, and loving, but when you get to know them, you wonder if they are even saved. It is the heart where the foundation is established, and it is there we must focus if we are to build a strong, stable, and lasting foundation for life.

In this chapter, we are going to center on how we can build and continue to build a strong spiritual foundation. Building a stable Christian life is not a one-time experience; it is a continuous process and work. It took time for Jesus to lay a foundation in the lives of His disciples so that they were grounded in His Word and understood His mission. After Jesus had established a strong foundation in His disciples, He also empowered them with the Holy Spirit so they could continue to build on that foundation and continue His work to the ends of the earth.

One thing spiritual builders must always remember is that Jesus must be the cornerstone of every spiritual foundation—not the traditions or wisdom of man but Jesus Himself. Most godly spiritual "parents" try to develop their spiritual children to be like them. There is nothing wrong with that, but Jesus must always be the only cornerstone. *Cornerstone* (see 1 Peter 2:6) refers to a capstone that holds an entire structure together. In ancient structures it was placed at a right angle joining two walls, and the royal name was inscribed on it to signify the ruler who took credit for the building's erection. When people try to take up the cornerstone position in the lives of their spiritual sons and daughters, they are simply taking the credit for themselves instead of giving God all the credit and glory. In addition, they are "cornerstones" that ultimately will fail; and when they fail, or make a mistake, their spiritual children likely will be disappointed, broken-hearted, and unhappy. But Jesus never fails. He is the Ancient of Days, the Creator, and the beginning and the end. Everything must begin with Him and end with Him.

As we build our spiritual life and help others do the same, we must remember that Jesus is the only cornerstone. That means He alone must be the capstone that holds together and gives focus to the life of every believer here on earth. We should help people become more like Christ, not more like us. We cannot sustain a spiritual life. Christ is the only chief cornerstone.

HOW TO BUILD

No person can build a strong spiritual life without a strong foundation; yet many people attempt to do that very thing. Why? People might not build a strong spiritual foundation because they want to save time and avoid the hard work it requires. Or perhaps they just want to join others who have already settled into a comfortable religious life that is built on a weak and unstable foundation. Or maybe they haven't heard about the violent storms that evil spiritual forces of this world unleash upon people at times. Whatever the reason, those who build cheap spiritual foundations or no foundation at all are shortsighted and one day will regret their failure. Building a strong spiritual foundation takes time, dedication, persistence, perseverance, and consistency.

To help us understand how to build a strong foundation in our lives, let us turn to 1 Kings.

> At the king's command they removed from the quarry large blocks of quality stone to provide a foundation of dressed stone for the temple. (1 Kings 5:17 NIV)
>
> The foundations were laid with large stones of good quality, some measuring ten cubits and some eight. (1 Kings 7:10 NIV)

The key to understanding the above texts is carefully looking at the function of each particular object mentioned. When we read a text like this, we tend to paint a mental picture of what the foundation will look like based on the description provided in the passage. That is not the goal of this passage, however; the aim of this passage simply is to illustrate the strength of the foundation because it was built using strong and costly materials. The role, or function, of these large blocks of quality stone was to provide the temple with a stable and solid foundation. These stones were not for decorative or appearance purposes.

God has given us His Son, His Word, His gifts, and His Holy Spirit to help us build a strong community of believers. However, we have to understand the role of each of these in our lives in order for us to fit perfectly in our position and become pillars in the body of Christ. They are not given to us for decorative purposes or so that we can brag about how knowledgeable or gifted or spiritual we are; they are freely given to us so we can build each other up (not tear each other down) and strengthen the body of Christ. How can we build our lives on the rock-solid foundation of Jesus Christ, and how do we know if we are His true followers? Luke 6:46–49 shows us how we can build our lives on Christ and how we can tell if we are His true disciples who are built on His foundation.

> "Why do you call me 'Lord, Lord,' and don't do the things I say? I will show you what someone is like who comes to me, hears my words, and acts on them: He is like a man building a house, who dug deep and laid the foundation on the rock. When the flood came, the river crashed against that house and couldn't shake it, because it was well built. But the one who hears and does not act is like a man who built a house on the ground without a foundation. The river crashed against it, and immediately it collapsed. And the destruction of that house was great!"

We can build our lives on the rock-solid foundation of Jesus Christ by being doers of His Word; and by being doers of His Word, we also demonstrate that we are His true followers. It is important to listen to the Word of God, but that is not enough; we also must obey His Word and do what it says. James 1:22 tells us to be doers of the Word and not just hearers. Only a person who has built his foundation on the Lord Jesus Christ is able to do what the Word of God says, for it is not an easy thing to obey the Word of God. A true disciple of Jesus Christ hears His Word, acts on His Word, and lets the Word of God bear fruit in his or her life.

Hearing the Word of God and doing what the Word says reveals a person's total dedication and devotion to the kingdom of heaven. To hear and not do the Word of God is very dangerous. It is like building our spiritual life on a sandy and weak foundation. Each time we hear the Word of God, we must do our best to walk in it and do it. Building a strong foundation takes time, endurance, perseverance, persistence, and dedication to the Word of God.

The costly materials *God* has provided to us for building strong foundations are His Son, Jesus Christ, His Word, and His Holy Spirit. The costly materials *we* have to sacrificially provide or contribute are obedience to the Word of God, a willing heart, fear of or reverence for God, commitment to prayer and to a local church, and faith, or trust, in Jesus Christ. The fear of the Lord in our lives is very important because the fear of the Lord is the basis of true knowledge (Proverbs 1:7). To fear God means to honor or reverence Him, to live in awe of His power, and to obey His Word. The fear of the Lord will help us stay true to the Word of God and not shift away from the hope we have in the good news of the kingdom. Our faith, or trust, in God will lead us to respect, honor, and love God wholeheartedly. It is our faith in Christ that keeps us focused on and dedicated to spiritual growth and maturity. When we pray in the Spirit, hear the Word of God, and obey it, we build up our spiritual lives. Prayer builds up not only our foundation in the Lord but also our relationship and fellowship with Him. It is costly to follow after Jesus, to walk faithfully with Him, to spend time with Him in prayer, to study His Word, and to do what His Word says to us; but these things are essential to a strong spiritual foundation.

TWO WAYS TO BUILD A HOUSE

In Luke 6:46–49 Jesus described to His disciples two ways to build a house. A person can build a house on a solid rock foundation or build without a foundation. In simplest terms, Jesus was driving home the point that anybody who claims to be His follower and yet does not obey His Word has not built his or her spiritual life on the solid rock foundation of Jesus Christ. Only the person who hears and does the Word of God has built his or her spiritual life on Christ. The interesting thing here is that Jesus had just been teaching about the fruit in people's lives. He stated, "A good tree doesn't produce bad fruit; on the other hand, a bad tree doesn't produce good fruit" (verse 43). And He said, "A good man produces good out of the good storeroom of his heart. An evil man produces evil out of the evil storeroom, for his mouth speaks from the overflow of the heart" (verse 45). Jesus was declaring that what is deep inside a person eventually will come out of that person.

Jesus' teaching about the production of a good or bad tree is directly connected to His teaching about the two different foundations. A good and well-established foundation can withstand the floodwaters, but a bad or nonexistent foundation cannot. In the strong foundation we see stability and firmness; in the other we see weakness and instability. The floodwaters are not able to break the house built on a solid rock foundation, for it is strong and immovable. Just as out of the storeroom of good comes good, out of a deeper and well-established foundation strength is produced. One cannot plant a bad tree and expect good fruit from it. The same is true with a foundation. You cannot lay a weak and shallow foundation and expect to have a strong house that can withstand the floodwaters. The strength of a house depends on the quality of the foundation that is beneath it. Your spiritual strength and your level of commitment to the Lord are totally dependent on the state or condition of your spiritual foundation.

UNLESS THE LORD BUILDS

> Unless the LORD builds a house, its builders labor over it in vain; unless the LORD watches over a city, the watchman stays alert in vain. In vain you get up early and stay up late, eating food earned by hard work; certainly He gives sleep to the one He loves. (Psalm 127:1–2)

The context or basic theme of Psalm 127 is that without the Lord's blessings all human toil is worthless. God is not against human effort; He honors hard work. However, any work that does not center on Him is worthless. These verses are a great reminder to the body of Christ that no task can succeed apart from God. As we desire to advance the kingdom of God and help people build their spiritual lives, we must remember that God is the one who builds people up according to His will, desire, and purpose. Teachers, pastors, and evangelists are there to lead people to the Architect Himself—God—who by the power of His Spirit then builds up a strong community of believers.

It is important to understand that building a strong and stable spiritual life can be achieved only by the power of God. That means we must submit our lives to Him so that through His Word He alone can build us up according to His plan, will, and purpose. Yes, builders of a house must labor over it, and watchmen of a city must stay awake and alert, but what guarantees the safety and protection of the house or the city is the all-powerful God. A life without God as the anchor or foundation can easily be shaken and destroyed by the power of the enemy. The secret to stability in life is to trust in God, the creator and giver of life. God is a builder; He is the only one who can build in us a strong spiritual foundation through His Word. That is why preachers must preach only the good news of the kingdom. It is the power that changes and transforms lives. And what God builds no one can destroy.

DESTROYING A WORLDLY FOUNDATION IN YOU

In order for God to build in us a new, sustainable, and strong spiritual foundation, we must first allow Him to destroy the old, worldly foundation in us through His Word and the power of His Spirit. A worldly foundation is simply a foundation that is centered on earthly, unspiritual, fleshly, and material things rather than on the things of God. Before a person is born again by the Spirit of God, his or her personal life is automatically built on a sinful and worldly foundation that Adam and Eve laid down for humanity. That means we do things in accordance with that foundation. However, when we give our lives to Jesus Christ and to His influence, we become a new people who must build our lives on Christ's foundation of righteousness. The problem many Christians have made is that they have simply attached Christ's foundation to their old, worldly, unspiritual foundation. They have made some improvements in many areas of their lives, but the old foundation is still present and still influencing their day-to-day lives.

A person with a worldly foundation is unstable in all his or her ways. This is because the person's foundation is built on insecurity, fear, jealousy, gossip, falsehood, ego, pride, anxiety, human wisdom, and selfishness. We can't be full of self and at the same time full of the Holy Spirit. In other words, we can't be full of worldliness and at the same time full of the kingdom of God. We are either in the kingdom of God, or we are not. We need to allow the Word of God and the Holy Spirit to destroy the worldly foundation and its influence on our lives. The Word of God is like fire and like a hammer (Jeremiah 23:29) that crushes the old foundation of our lives. Adam and Eve's fall not only allowed sin to enter the world but also established a sinful foundation. Today we are born with a sinful nature because of the foundation set before us by Adam and Eve. However, Jesus' death and resurrection overturned that foundation. He set a good and new foundation upon which people can safely build their lives.

Compelled by His love and mercy, God sent His only Son, Jesus Christ, to secure salvation and establish a new, strong, and solid foundation for all who trust in Him. Establishing this new platform or foundation for mankind cost Him His only Son. Freedom is not free; it is costly. Building a new house, or in this instance a new community of believers, cost God something. The blood of Jesus Christ has redeemed us because God was willing to pay the price for each one of us. There is no need for us Christians to remain chained to our past and to the influence of this world. We have been set free to live a free but costly life in Christ and for His kingdom. We must let go of our old worldly foundation if we are to see more of the glory and power of God in our lives and in the church. There is only one foundation that can hold our lives together, and that foundation is the Lord Jesus Christ. At all cost we must let God deal with our personal lives at a foundational level so that we can flourish and shine with the presence and power of God. Our personal spiritual foundation must be built upon the wisdom of God and not upon the wisdom of this world.

> Trust in the Lord with all your heart, and do not rely on your own understanding; think about Him in all your ways, and He will guide you on the right paths. (Proverbs 3:5–6)

Building a godly foundation is costly, as we have already stated. It was costly to God, and building a spiritual foundation on the foundation He laid will cost you as well. It will cost you your pride, ego, time, and will.

But in return you will have a stable life that can never be moved, and you will become strength to the weak and a channel through which God can touch the nations and transform lives. The fear (awe or reverence) of God will govern your life and activities, which means that everything you do or desire to do will be to God's glory and honor. One who builds on a worldly foundation is full of anxiety, bitterness, pride, self-seeking, competition, unforgiveness, gossip, anger, and ungodliness; but the one with a godly foundation is born again (John 3:3). That person is no longer bound to the influence of the sinful nature (Romans 8:9), and the Spirit of Christ resides in his heart (Galatians 4:6). The old has gone, and the new has come (2 Corinthians 5:17); and he is joyful, loving, peaceful, kind, faithful, and patient (Galatians 5:22–23).

The reason many Christians continue living a lifestyle that does not demonstrate the nature of Christ is that they are still under the influence of the old, worldly foundation. How can a Christian who claims to have the character of Christ in him or her hate another Christian? First John 4:20 tells us, "If anyone boasts, 'I love God,' and goes right on hating his brother or sister, thinking nothing of it, he is a liar. If he won't love the person he can see, how can he love the God he can't see?" (MSG).

It is amazing to see that when a Christian brother or sister—for whatever reason—leaves a local church, often other members of that church, including some "leaders," immediately stop talking to that sister or brother. This simply demonstrates that the spirit of the world sometimes has more influence on Christians than does the Spirit of Jesus Christ. Those who build their spiritual foundation on the foundation of Christ will exhibit His nature and characteristics. He loves people, and nothing can change His love for them, whether they are in His kingdom or outside His kingdom. He hates the sin in people, but He loves people. We must learn to love other Christians whether or not they belong to the same congregation we do.

In the next chapter, we are going to look at the influence of a foundation for "good" or "bad." The old foundation will always attempt to rise up and keep you bound as a captive to its influence and ways, but you must boldly declare that your past nature is gone and the new has come. Christ has set you free from the shackles and power of the past; you are a new creation, created with a new mind and heart and with the spirit of Christ. You love as He loves, you care for people as He cares, you forgive as He forgives, and you give as He gives.

In order for us to move forward in the Lord and effectively do the business of the kingdom of God here and now, we need to allow the Holy Spirit to destroy the old, worldly foundation in us so that we can confidently say, "I have been crucified with Christ and I no longer live, but Christ lives in me. The life I live in the body, I live by faith in the Son of God, who loved me and gave himself for me" (Galatians 2:20 NIV).

CHAPTER 6

The Influence of A Foundation

A personal spiritual foundation has great influence in a person's life. People's actions, attitudes, behavior, and character come from the foundation of their lives. The base of your life is the source of everything about you—what you think and how you think and what you do and how you do it. Your words and behavior simply demonstrate the condition of the foundation you have built in your heart and reveal your belief system, or ideology. That is why it is false to claim that your life is founded on Christ's foundation or principles if the things you do or say do not demonstrate the character of Jesus Christ. If you are standing on the biblical foundation of Jesus Christ, you must be able to demonstrate the influence of Christ's distinctive nature in your life.

Christ's unique nature in us is what causes us to be a people *in* this world but not *of* this world. That means we do things differently from the rest of the world, and we see things differently from how the rest of the world sees them. The God in us is not the god of this world. This isn't to say that when we come to Christ we must be perfect, of course, but something in the heart must change and continue to change. If nothing is changing in us, then we have personally chosen not to change anything. We have the power to allow a higher level of transformation by the Spirit of God in our life or to prevent that transformation from taking place. We have the power to grow spiritually or not grow spiritually. Our desire, passion, zeal, and dedication to the Word of God can be hindered by our past foundation if we do not deal with it. God is a God who always looks and moves forward, not backward. He wants us to move forward too.

> Do not remember the past events, pay no attention to things of old. Look, I am about to do something new; even now it is coming. Do you not see it? Indeed, I will make a way in the wilderness, rivers in the desert. (Isaiah 43:18–19)

Through Isaiah the prophet, God told the Jewish exiles they should not live in the past but look forward to God's delivering them from Babylon through another exodus by making a way in the wilderness. The past miracles were nothing compared to what God was going to do for them in the future. God does not work in the past; He works in the now and in the future. Don't get stuck in the past. Don't look to the past. The past can kill you or kill your future. The account of Lot's wife in Genesis 19:23–26 clearly illustrates how looking to the past when God has commanded you to move forward can kill you.

In Genesis 19 we read about Sodom and Gomorrah's wickedness and God's plans to demolish these cities. Before God would destroy these cities, He sent His angels to instruct Lot to take his wife and his two daughters out of the city. When Lot hesitated to leave the city, the angels grabbed Lot's hand, his wife's hand, and the hands of his daughters and led them out of the city (verses 15–16). One of the angels instructed them to run for their lives toward the mountains and not look back or stop (verse 17). Lot's wife ignored God's instruction; she looked back, and immediately she became a pillar of salt. The disobedience of Lot's wife brought about one of the most puzzling deaths in all of human history, as she *became* a pillar of salt. By looking back to the city, Lot's wife demonstrated that she was still clinging to the past. Her heart and mind were still in the city, even though her body had physically left it. Many Christians have physically left the things of the past, but deep down in their hearts and minds they are still controlled by them.

You can't make any progress with God as long as you are still holding on to some pieces of your old life. Most Christians are like Lot's wife: they are willing to go forward but are not willing to let go of their past. They want the past to go with them into the future. With God there is no mixing the two; the past is the past, and the new is new.

The Spirit and power of God in us are limited when we allow the things of the past to get into our new foundation in Christ. The things we allow into our heart influence our decisions and actions. In Mark 7:18–23 Jesus explained that what comes out of a person is what defiles the person. He said, "For from within, out of people's hearts, come evil thoughts, sexual immoralities, thefts, murders, adulteries, greed, evil actions, deceit, lewdness, stinginess, blasphemy, pride, and foolishness. All these evil things come from within and defile a person" (verses 21–23).

As the context of this passage shows, the Jews of Jesus' day believed they could be clean before God simply by following the dietary laws of Leviticus 11 and observing various washings taught by the rabbis. Even Peter struggled with this (Acts 10:9–29). But Jesus pointed out that sin begins in the attitudes and intentions of the inner person. Jesus was more concerned about the heart than about food laws. What we put into our minds through reading, hearing, or watching is what either corrupts or nourishes our spiritual lives.

A defiled foundation (heart) produces the defiled things mentioned in Mark 7:21–22. What is in us is what we will produce; we cannot produce what is not in us. If Christ is truly in you and He is the anchor of your life, you will produce the spirit of Christ. If you feed your mind and your heart with junk such as hatred, unforgiveness, bitterness, and jealousy, you will become spiritually obese with the spirit of the world.

In 1 Samuel 17 we see a young and inexperienced David challenge the mighty giant Goliath. The question many of us don't ask is this: What led the young man David to step up to the plate and challenge the mighty Goliath? For forty days Goliath mocked the army of Israel, and yet the army of Israel could not do anything about it. But when the young David heard Goliath taunting Israel's army, something inside of him was stirred up; and David asked the soldiers standing nearby, "What shall be done for the man who kills this Philistine and takes away the reproach from Israel? For who is this uncircumcised Philistine, that he should defy the armies of the living God?" (1 Samuel 17:26).

THE POWER OF A CHILDHOOD FOUNDATION

The influence of honor and reverence for the name of the living God in David's heart caused him to challenge the unchallenged Goliath. David's foundation of faith and trust in the name of Yahweh also played a big part. Because of his deep faith in the power of God, David stated to Goliath, "I come to you in the name of the LORD of hosts, the God of the armies of Israel, whom you have defied" (1 Samuel 17:45).

When honor, reverence, and love for God are in your heart, you can boldly defend the name of God. The foundation upon which your life stands can help you move forward in life, or it can move you backward. It is important to establish a godly foundation in your life and rid yourself of your past foundation so that it does not become an obstacle to where God wants to take you. In the next few pages, we are going to look at the power of a childhood foundation. It is important for parents, as well as spiritual fathers and mothers, to make sure they help their children establish a foundation that is built on Christ and His Word. It is also important that adult Christians learn to deal properly with their pasts and move forward with a strong spiritual foundation.

A childhood foundation has a greater effect on us than most of us realize. Indeed, our childhood experiences, good or bad, have a tremendous impact on our adulthood and spiritual life. They have the power to shape our personality in a good or a bad way. Setting up a new foundation in our life requires us to forget about past memories and problems and to forgive people and be forgiven by people so that we can enter into a new season of life with a new spirit.

Things we go through in life may directly or indirectly build up a foundation in our lives. This foundation may either hinder us or empower us to move forward in life. People who have experienced lawlessness or trauma often struggle with trusting people because somebody they trusted abused them and laid a foundation of mistrust. The church is full of people who struggle to trust each other because of their past experiences in life. That is one reason it can be so difficult for the people of God to work together in unity and advance the kingdom of God. As spiritual as people may look, many struggle with childhood experiences that affect their spiritual growth and maturity and the effectiveness of the church.

Proverbs 22:6 says, "Train up a child in the way he should go; even when he is old he will not depart from it" (ESV). This Proverb echoes Genesis 18:19: "For I have chosen him, that he may command his children and his household after him to keep the way of the LORD by doing righteousness and justice, so that the LORD may bring to Abraham what he has promised him" (ESV).

The word translated "train up" in Proverbs 22:6 literally means to "devote" or "initiate" someone or give someone necessary preparation so that he or she may reach the standard required to function in a particular role. The Hebrew words translated "in the way he should go" speak of orienting the initiation to fit the challenges of young people.[3] Training up someone is preparing that person for the future and the challenges of it. When a child is trained up in the ways and things of God, a foundation is laid down in that child's life so that "when he is old he will not depart from it."

When a childhood foundation has been properly set up in a person's life through the Word of God, it becomes that person's very nature and thus almost impossible to obliterate. It is also true that when a bad foundation based on bad experiences and memories has been established in a person's life, it is almost impossible to demolish that foundation. Most people who have had bad childhood experiences struggle to love and forgive and to move forward in life because the foundation of their childhood has kept them in captivity. Jesus Christ is able to release people from such captivity. No matter how ugly your past may be, remember this: Jesus Christ has the power to cut it off from you and to give you a fresh beginning. Don't

---

[3] Howard, ed., *HCSB Study Bible,* 1067, note on Proverbs 22:6.

let the burden of your past keep you from moving forward. Surrender it all to the Lord Jesus Christ.

> "Come to me, all of you who are weary and burdened, and I will give you rest. All of you, take up my yoke and learn from me. Because I am gentle and humble in heart, and you will find rest for yourselves. For My yoke is easy and my burden is light." (Matthew 11:28–30)

A yoke is a heavy wooden harness that fits over the shoulders of oxen. It is then attached to whatever the oxen are pulling. Many people carry heavy burdens of childhood rejection, mistreatment, sin, bitterness, and pain. These burdens have the power to shape people's lives and relationships with others for the rest of their lives. The Word of God, the good news of the kingdom that Jesus preached, is able to set people free from the power of the past and give them a new beginning and an easy burden. Jesus' yoke of discipleship brings freedom and rest through simple commitment to Him (1 John 5:3).

> "The Spirit of the Lord is on me, because He has anointed me to preach good news to the poor. He has sent me to proclaim freedom to the captives and recovery of sight to the blind, to set free the oppressed, to proclaim the year of the Lord's favor." (Luke 4:18)

The greatest mission of Jesus Christ is to set people free from their captivity and oppression. Whatever forms of captivity or oppression you may be experiencing, Jesus is here to set you free.

Not only does the past keep people in captivity, but it also torments and oppresses them. Even the good memories of the past can keep people in captivity and stop them from moving forward in life. When God says move forward, we must move forward, forgetting what is behind us, whether good or bad, and enter into His new promises.

Paul wrote in Philippians 3:13–14, "Brothers, I do not consider myself to have taken hold of it. But one thing I do: Forgetting what is behind and reaching forward to what is ahead, I pursue as my goal the prize promised by God's heavenly call in Christ Jesus." The key in this scripture is "forgetting what is behind." Forgetting the past isn't easy, but it must be done in order to press forward and take hold of what God has prepared for us.

Chapter 7

Revisiting Our Spiritual Foundation

A house that is crooked and twisted out of shape is unstable, unreliable, and dangerous to live in because it can fall apart at any time. To fix such a house, you need to fix its foundation first. Painting it or decorating it will not do if the house stands on a twisted foundation, for as beautiful as it might look, it still will be washed away when the floodwaters come. Sadly, the religious system in the Christian world today has corrupted and twisted God's design and purposes. As a result, many lives, marriages, and churches are unstable. We have built our lives on a corrupt and unsustainable foundation. Jesus Christ is the only foundation, and if He is not the foundation on which we build our lives, everything in our lives is going to be in complete disorder and confusion. Colossians 1:17 says, "He is before all things, and in him all things hold together" (NIV). Jesus is the only foundation that sustains and holds everything together. In Him our lives and marriages are held together, protected, and prevented from disintegrating into complete disorder.

Many Christians are struggling both spiritually and physically, and they do not know why. People with good intentions and a desire to live for God end up doing things they don't like doing—namely, sin. Others find that even after a powerful service or prayer meeting, they end up in the same mud they have been trying to get out of. At this point people often begin to look for someone to blame for their instability. If it is not the pastor's fault for not preaching a powerful message, it is the Devil's fault. Some even go to the extent of blaming God Himself. God is not the problem, and our friends and families are not the problem. We are each responsible for how we build our lives in the Lord and respond to the power of the good news of the kingdom. The desires of the flesh disturb the desires of the Spirit of God in us, and that is why we do what we hate doing.

In Romans 7:15–20 Paul had this to say:

> For I do not understand what I am doing, because I do not practice what I want to do, but I do what I hate. And if I do what I do not want to do, I agree with the law that it is good. So now I am no longer the one doing it, but it is sin living in me. For I know that nothing good lives in me, that is, in my flesh. For the desire to do what is good is with me, but there is no ability to do it. For I do not do the good that I want to do, but I practice the evil that I do not want to do. Now if I do what I do not want, I am no longer the one doing it, but it is the sin that lives in me.

There are many different views and interpretations of this passage. To understand this difficult and controversial passage in the letter to the Romans, we need first to discover what this man's problem really was. What made him do the things he hated doing? In verse 14 he stated, "The law is spiritual; but I am made out of flesh." Galatians 5:19–20 tells us that the works of the flesh are sexual immorality, impurity, sensuality, idolatry, sorcery, enmity, strife, jealousy, fits of anger, rivalries, dissensions, divisions, envy, drunkenness, and orgies. The problem Paul was trying to point out here was the power of the flesh. As long as we are living in the flesh and not in the Spirit, the flesh has the power to make us do the things of the flesh.

The only Person who can overcome the power and influence of the flesh in us is the Holy Spirit. Again, Paul wrote,

> I say then, walk by the Spirit and you will not carry out the desire of the flesh. For the flesh desires what is against

> the Spirit, and the Spirit desires what is against the flesh; these are opposed to each other, so that you don't do what you want. But if you are led by the Spirit, you are not under the law. (Galatians 5:16–18)

When the desires of the flesh have the upper hand in a person's life, the works of the flesh are obvious and visible. In the same way, when the desires of the Spirit have the upper hand in a person's life, the fruit of the Spirit is visible. Most of us do the things we hate doing simply because we have knowingly or unknowingly built our lives on the foundation of the flesh rather than on the foundation of Christ and the Spirit of God. That is why we are full of bitterness, jealousy, unforgiveness, division, selfish ambition, hatred, and similar things. Because of the influence of the flesh, we are unable to sustain the move of God, advance the kingdom of God, or work together in unity.

Why should we revisit our spiritual foundation? First of all, to "revisit" simply means to look at something again or to reexamine something. In this case we are revisiting or reexamining our spiritual foundation with a view to making a fresh start in our Christian lives and fellowship with God and with each other. The more we stand on Christ's foundation, the more we are able to do the will of God and the business of the kingdom of heaven. Galatians 5:24 tells us, "Now those who belong to Christ Jesus have crucified the flesh with its passions and desires." We need to reexamine our lives and make sure the flesh is crucified and not standing in the way of the fresh anointing God desires to pour out on His church today.

We all need to revisit the spiritual foundation of our lives if we are to avoid doing the things we hate doing. The flesh is hostile to the things of the Spirit. As long as the flesh is dominant in our lives, we will continue living in the same spiritual condition and religious system. God does not want us to be content to remain there. As a new generation, with a new heart and spirit, we first must desire to change the spiritual state of our lives. God wants us to move forward and walk with Him and in Him. Only then can we have an impact on the nations of the world. We need to revisit the entire spiritual system and usher in the system of the kingdom of heaven to rule and reign in the church today so that we can demonstrate its character and nature.

Satan's goal is to tamper with our spiritual foundation, which is the source or center of our belief, faith, stability, and trust in God. If he can manage to get us even slightly off our foundation in Christ, he can then mislead, manipulate, and deceive us and pull us away from the presence of God. Many people who were once on fire, passionate, and zealous for God are no longer on fire today because they allowed the enemy to interfere with the foundation. To keep the fire of God burning in our lives, we need to be diligent doers of the Word of God. This is not easy, but with sheer determination and with the help of the Holy Spirit, we can do it. Ultimately, what keeps us on fire for God is a right foundation. The church in general has lost the fire of God because the people of God have become lukewarm. No matter how hard we preach revival, teach revival, and speak revival, if the people don't have a foundation for revival to take place, nothing tangible will happen.

What we need is a new foundation, a new beginning in Christ and with Christ. When we draw near to God, He will draw near to us and cause us to walk in His power and presence. He is all we need, not another program or system but God alone, because He is the one who makes everything successful. Anything to do with God begins and ends with God. If we need revival or a great move of God, we need to go back to Him; otherwise, all we will be doing is playing church, and a religious game can never transform lives or change the world.

Chapter 8

Fight To Rebuild Your Life

Rebuilding your life or shifting your mind-set from a worldly centered lifestyle to a godly, or kingdom, way of living isn't easy. It requires passion, dedication, persistence, and the renewing of your mind on a daily basis through the Holy Spirit (Romans 12:1–2). Many people find it very difficult to build or rebuild their new life in Christ because of opposition. Opposition will always be there because the enemy does not want to see people build their lives according to God's design and purpose. Your passion and dedication, together with the power of prayer, can overcome such opposition. Your desire to live according to God's will and purpose must be the driving force to rebuild your life in the midst of opposition. The enemy will try to keep you in bondage and captivity by reminding you of your past mistakes and instilling fear in you. Fear is one of the greatest weapons the enemy uses to stop people from moving forward and rebuilding their spiritual lives. However, when you have a passion to change the history and direction of your life or of a nation, fear and opposition have no power over you because God is your strength.

The account of Nehemiah's rebuilding the broken-down walls of Jerusalem helps us see what passionate people can do. Nehemiah was a cupbearer to King Artaxerxes of Persia. After learning that the walls of Jerusalem were in ruins and the city's (fortified) gates had been destroyed by fire, Nehemiah sat down and wept and mourned for days and fasted and prayed to the God of heaven (Nehemiah 1:4). He went to the king and asked him for permission to return to Jerusalem to rebuild the walls (Nehemiah 2:5).

The king granted him his request (verse 6), and the challenging task of rebuilding the broken-down walls began. Notice that Nehemiah did not play the blame game, wait for someone else to do something, or just talk about the broken-down walls, as many of us would do. He took personal responsibility for turning the situation around.

OVERCOMING OPPOSITION WITH PRAYER

When Sanballat the Horonite and Tobiah the Ammonite and Geshem the Arab heard about Nehemiah's mission to rebuild the walls and help the people of Israel, they were very displeased (Nehemiah 2:10, 19). So they mocked and despised Nehemiah and his people and accused them of rebelling against the king (Nehemiah 2:19). They said the damage was too extensive and the walls could never be rebuilt. And as Nehemiah and the people he had assembled to rebuild the walls began the work, Tobiah the Ammonite ridiculed them, saying, "That stone wall would collapse if even a fox walked along the top of it" (Nehemiah 4:3 NLT).

Nehemiah did not go after the people who were making fun of them; instead, he prayed to the God of heaven:

> Hear us, our God, for we are being mocked. May their scoffing fall back on their own heads, and may they themselves become captives in a foreign land! Do not ignore their guilt. Do not blot out their sins, for they have provoked you to anger here in front of the builders. (Nehemiah 4:4–5 NLT)

The people worked with enthusiasm, and the walls were completed to half their height around the entire city. When their enemies saw this, they were furious and made plans to go and fight against Jerusalem and throw the people into confusion. But the people again prayed to their God and guarded the city day and night to protect themselves (Nehemiah 4:7–9).

Then another problem arose when the people themselves began to complain that they were getting too tired and there was too much rubble to move. They became convinced they could not build the walls by themselves, and they were frightened by their enemies' threats of violence (Nehemiah 4:10–11). Nehemiah responded by placing guards to secure the work and the people and encouraging his people not to be afraid of the enemy. He said to them, "Remember the Lord, who is great and glorious, and fight for your friends, your families, and your homes!" (Nehemiah 4:14 NLT).

The work of rebuilding the walls was opposed at all levels, but with the help of God and the builders' persistence, the work was finally completed after just fifty-two days (Nehemiah 6:15). Because of Nehemiah's dedication to rebuilding the broken-down walls, the enemies' opposition and threats of attack were not allowed to stop the rebuilding project. Nehemiah was a man of character, persistence, and prayer. When he heard about the ruined walls of Jerusalem, he did not just sit down and do nothing about it. He took full responsibility and identified himself with the sin of his people, confessing to God, "Both I and my father's house have sinned." He recognized the problem, responded to the problem with prayer, and then acted on the problem. Prayer is still God's weapon in solving problems. Through prayer God reveals His plans, gives guidance, and empowers His people to accomplish His mission.

Often, we Christians are quick to say the church is in bad shape or the body of Christ needs revival, and yet we sit and do nothing about it. It is very easy to analyze, scrutinize, and point out the problems in the church, as well as in the world, but God is looking for people like Nehemiah, people who will not just discuss a situation but will fight to do something about it. Nehemiah saw a problem and was distressed about it. But instead of complaining or blaming it on the sins of the people, he cried out to God for forgiveness and restored the walls of Jerusalem while standing firm against the opposition.

As we rebuild our spiritually broken lives, we will face opposition and mockery from those who would rather see us remain in bondage. We must passionately fight to rebuild our lives through the power of prayer so that we can live according to God's plans. Before we can rebuild the church and restore her position in the community, we first need to rebuild our lives spiritually. But God is counting on us to change the spiritual condition of the church. The church's current spiritual condition in the world should move our hearts to cry out to God, to repent of our sins, and to act upon the problems the church is facing. This task may seem difficult; but under God's direction and power, we can accomplish the impossible.

Instead of just talking about the problems in your local church or in the world, become a vessel God can use to bring reformation to the church and the world. People will oppose you, call you a rebel and radical, and attempt to demoralize you, but you must be willing to lay your life down for the sake of God's kingdom. Most Bible characters who made a difference and changed the history of the church endured hardships, persecution, and opposition because they set themselves apart for the sake of the kingdom of heaven. It is important to understand that before God can radically change the world, He has to radically change His people first. Change begins with us, the "temple" of God.

We must fight to rebuild our spiritual lives so that we can be part of the glorious church God is building for His glory. Even though the church belongs to God and Jesus Christ is the head over it, the strength and stability of a church in any given community is dependent on the strength and stability of the people who make up that church. It is vitally important for all of us to have a right foundation in place so that we can function as living stones in the house of God and not dead stones. God even now is in the business of restoring His house (church) and His people to His original intent. The church is due for a fresh anointing, mandate, and direction from God. And the time is right for God's people to rediscover the purpose and vision of God for His house.

God works with people to achieve His goals and vision. But those who desire to be used by Him first must empty themselves and put their lives and households in order so that they can reveal the glory and presence of God. The church is not a building; we, the people of God, are the church. God wants to work with each one of us to fill this earth with His glory and power.

In the next chapter, we are going to look at the church God is building in the world today through His people. He is positioning and setting apart a new generation He will use to rebuild His house on the earth.

Chapter 9

The Church God Is Building

The church God is building in the world today through His Son Jesus Christ is different from the lukewarm, prayerless, and powerless churches we have all seen and experienced. He is building a house of healing, a vibrant, glory-filled church that is united with Him in the task of filling the earth with His glory, a church that is alive and passionate for what God is passionate for: the hurting world, hurting people, and perishing souls. God is setting apart leaders who have a heart for His Word and His vision for the people. The church is central to God's mighty work on the earth. The church is the agent of the kingdom of God, and the church's mandate is to set the captives free and to house the glory and presence of God. When the church is not doing very well, society and nations suffer.

Many people are rightly crying out to God to send revival, but it is important to understand that before God can send His revival, He must restore the church to her original state. True revival comes after restoration. God is a God of order, and He must set things in order before He can breathe His life into His church. Restoration involves the work of repairing, fixing, mending, rebuilding, remodeling, revamping, and making things over again. God is restoring His church to His original intention for her. There have been many different "revivals" in the world, but very few of them last, or have lasted, for very long. When God lights up His fire, it burns until everything turns to ashes. He doesn't just light up the fire because the people want the fire; He lights His fire when the people are ready, in unity, with one mind, one voice, and one vision for setting the world on fire for Him.

Before Jesus allowed His disciples to leave Jerusalem and be His witnesses in Judea and Samaria and to the ends of the earth, He instructed them to wait for the power of the Holy Spirit (Acts 1:4–8). In Acts 1:12–14 we see His disciples united in prayer, and in verses 15–26, we see them setting their house in order by choosing a disciple (Matthias) to replace Judas. In Acts 2:1–4, when the day of Pentecost arrived, all the believers were meeting together in one place. Suddenly, there was a sound from heaven like the roaring of a mighty windstorm, and it filled the house where they were sitting. Then, what looked like flames or tongues of fire appeared and settled on each of them. And everyone present was filled with the Holy Spirit and began speaking in other languages, as the Holy Spirit gave them this ability.

Once the people were united and ready, God did His part by pouring out the power of His Holy Spirit upon them. He set them on fire to testify to and proclaim the power of the good news of the kingdom. They had to be ready first before they could be unleashed to transform lives. Fire is a symbol of God's purifying presence. He had to purify these disciples first and burn away the undesirable elements in their lives and set their hearts aflame to ignite the lives of the people in Jerusalem, Judea, Samaria, and the ends of the earth.

The point here is that before God sends His reviving fire upon the church today, He is going to raise up and empower men and women who will first rebuild the broken-down walls of the church and put the church in order. There is too much disorder and disunity in the body of Christ today, and we who are members of this body have caused this disorder. The church is not the building we meet in. We the people are the church; and if we are dysfunctional in any way, the entire church also will be dysfunctional. The seven churches mentioned in Revelation 2–3 give us an idea of what the church God is delighted in and building on the earth looks like. They also give us a picture of the kinds of churches that are currently operating in the world today.

When we look at five of the seven churches of Revelation, we immediately see the good things they were doing. Those churches probably were shocked, however, when Jesus, the head of the church, examined them and found them severely lacking. The **Ephesus Church** (Revelation 2:1–7) was commended for her hard work, patient endurance, and zero tolerance for false teachers, but the believers there had lost their love for the Lord and for each other. Every hard work for the kingdom of God must spring from love for Jesus Christ and for His people.

The **Smyrna Church** (2:8–11) suffered persecution and poverty. Jesus found no problem with this church. Instead, He encouraged these believers not to fear what the enemy was going to do to them but to remain faithful to the point of death. The **Pergamum Church** (2:12–17) was commended for remaining loyal to the Lord in a city where Satan's influence was strong. The believers experienced great pressure to compromise or abandon their faith, but they stood their ground and refused to deny the Lord. Yet they tolerated those who, like Balaam, led people away from God.

The **Thyatira Church** (2:18–29) was praised for love, faithfulness, service, and patient endurance. The church had grown in good deeds and was constantly improving, but the people had permitted a woman to teach that sexual immorality was not a serious matter for believers. The **Sardis Church** (3:1–6) was a superficial church that had a reputation for being spiritually alive, yet the church actually was spiritually dead. Jesus instructed the believers in Sardis to go back to what they had first heard and believed. The **Philadelphia Church** (3:7–13) was a church of little or limited strength, and yet the people were faithful and obedient to the Word of God. Jesus encouraged them to hold tightly to whatever strength they had. And, finally, the **Laodicea Church** (3:14–22) was neither hot nor cold. This was a lukewarm church that never stood up for anything.

If Jesus were to visit His churches today, very few would be compared to the Philadelphia or Smyrna churches. Most churches are like the other five churches—doing many things right but missing the mark and the vision of God for His church. We need to go back to the good news of the kingdom to rediscover our mission and calling.

THE CHURCH IS NOT THE BUILDING

It is important to understand that the church is not the building but a group of people who believe in God and are joined together in Him. Ephesians 2:20–21 says, "We are his house, built on the foundation of the apostles and the prophets. And the cornerstone is Christ Jesus himself. We who believe are carefully joined together, becoming a holy temple for the Lord" (NLT). Most people, Christians included, tend to think of the church as a mere building in which people meet. But according to Paul, the church is not a building; the people are the church, and they have a distinctive foundation. The church is built on the foundation of the apostles and prophets, and Jesus is the cornerstone.

There are several views and interpretations regarding the apostles and prophets being the foundation of the church in view of the fact that Jesus is also said to be the foundation of the church and the capstone that holds the church together. Paul may have been referring to the intensive founding work of the early Christian apostles and prophets as they taught and proclaimed Jesus Christ the promised Messiah. In Matthew 16:15, Jesus asked His disciples, "Who do you say that I am?" Peter responded, "You are the Messiah, the Son of the living God!" (verse 16). In verses 17–18 Jesus responded to Peter with these words:

> "Simon son of Jonah, you are blessed because flesh and blood did not reveal this to you, but My Father in heaven. And I also say to you that you are Peter, and on this rock I will build My church, and the forces of Hades will not overpower it."

Peter's proclamation of Jesus' messiahship laid the foundation for the church. Many people had rejected Jesus. They could not believe that He was indeed the promised Messiah because they were expecting a Messiah who would be a military deliverer. Even Jesus' disciples were slow to understand the nature of His messiahship. The apostles and prophets are the "foundation" of the church in the sense that they faithfully taught that

Jesus Christ is the Messiah and the Son of God. This basic truth is essential to the church and the Christian life.

The church is a people, or a community of believers, who are filled with the Holy Spirit and empowered to live in unity with one another and to demonstrate the heart of God. Whenever you go to a place of worship, bear in mind that you are the church. Do your best to be the church Jesus would attend and be a part of.

In 1 Corinthians 3:16–17 Paul said to the believers in Corinth, "Don't you realize that all of you together are the temple of God and that the Spirit of God lives in you? God will bring ruin upon anyone who ruins this temple. For God's temple is holy, and you Christians are that temple" (NLT). The first thing we notice here is that Paul called the believers at Corinth corporately "the temple of God" and said "the Spirit of God" lived in them. In the Old Testament, God had the temple for His earthly "residence," but now He has believers in Christ as His residence, or dwelling place. The corporate body or assembly of believers at Corinth was a "temple" built by God, and His Spirit resided among them.

The importance of the "temple" in the Hebrew Scriptures (Old Testament) did not rest in its immense value due to its ornate construction, but rather in the presence and glory of God that dwelt in the temple. Great care was given to its design, and immense wealth was contained in the building materials because it was to be the house or dwelling place for the *shekinah* glory of God. The church is not the church without God's presence and God's people. In 1 Corinthians 6:19–20 Paul wrote to the Corinthian assembly:

> Or don't you know that your body is the temple of the Holy Spirit, who lives in you and was given to you by God? You do not belong to yourself, for God bought you with a high price. So you must honor God with your body. (NLT)

The Spirit of God lives within each one of us, making our body a temple of God's presence. Many Christians use their bodies any way they want, not realizing they are carrying the Spirit of the living God inside them. The more we realize we are the church and the church is us, the more we will desire to be the church God wants to establish on the earth. In addition, we will also aspire to be stable ambassadors of the kingdom of God. When the world looks at the church, they don't look at the "building" but at the lifestyle or heart of us, the people who represent God in His house. And if we who represent God in society are unstable and unloving, how can we convince the world we are the true children of God? Jesus said in John 13:35, "Your love for one another will prove to the world that you are my disciples" (NLT).

THE STRENGTH AND POWER OF A CORPORATE BODY

Reconciliation, care, honor for God and for each other, the presence and glory of God, healing, unity, and love for one another and for God are some of the distinguishing marks of the church God is building in this generation. Christlike love will prove to the world that we are Jesus' disciples, a chosen people, a royal priesthood, a holy nation, and God's possession. The current body of Christ is filled with the spirit of division, hatred for one another, competition, and individualism. Consequently, the church is weak. We need to evaluate our spiritual lives and change the way we think so that we can be the church that can demonstrate the true character and nature of God to the hurting world.

When an individual's spiritual foundation is strong, the body of Christ becomes stronger and the community of believers becomes functional. It is important to know that in order for a corporate body to function powerfully, each individual must establish a firm foundation in his or her life. When believers in Christ come together and are united as one body with one purpose, the body of Christ will move forward because there is great power in unity. The corporate body is only as strong as the individuals who make up the body. Pastors, leaders, and followers must realize that the church is not a one-man show but a united, corporate body where each and every one is doing something within his or her area of gifting. Each person has a duty and role to play in the body of Christ.

Instead of pointing fingers and blaming one another for the absence of the power and presence of God in our churches today, we should humble ourselves and unite to rebuild our broken spiritual system so that we can have a new beginning in the Lord and be the church God is building. The present spiritual condition of the church can be fixed if each one of us will take responsibility for building a new spiritual foundation in our lives that rests on the foundation of Christ and the principles of His kingdom.

In Galatians 2:19–20 Paul declared, "I have been crucified with Christ. I myself no longer live, but Christ lives in me. So I live my life in this earthly body by trusting in the Son of God, who loved me and gave himself for me" (NLT). In order for the church to function properly as a corporate body and walk in the power of God, our old self must be crucified with Christ so that we no longer live according to the influence of that old "self" but according to Christ's character and kingdom. Paul's statement, "I have been crucified," signaled a new beginning. The way he used to be or do things died on the cross with Jesus, and his new life was now based on a new foundation of faith in Christ. By dying to our old self or life, we begin a new Christian life that is united not only with Christ but also with other believers in Christ.

The days of pulpit revival and the spirit of individualism are coming to an end. God is ushering in the strength and power of a corporate body. Who can stop a united front? The account of the Tower of Babel, or Babylon, in Genesis 11:1–9 shows us what a united people can do. Even though the people who built the tower were united for the wrong reason, we can learn from them the power and force of unity. The people were united by the same language and the same desire.

> And they said, "Come, let us build ourselves a city and a tower with its top in the sky. Let us make a name for ourselves; otherwise, we will be scattered over the face of the whole earth." Then the LORD came down to look over the city and the tower that the men were building. The LORD said, "If, as one people all having the same

> language, they have begun to do this, then nothing they plan to do will be impossible for them."

God recognized the power of unity these people possessed because they had one language and one mind-set; so He stopped them by confusing them with different languages. After this confusion of languages, the people could no longer build the Tower of Babel, probably because they could not understand each other anymore.

Imagine, though, if Christians came together united with one voice, one mind, and one heart for the purpose of advancing the kingdom of God. What could stop us or stand in our way?

The enemy knows full well what the people of God can do in unity. That is why he seeks to bring division into the church. Division is one of the biggest hindrances to the progress of the work of God in the world. Disunity in the body of Christ not only hinders the progress of the work of God but also prevents the power and presence of God from being manifested in a powerful way. The power of "all" is very important in this time we are living in and crucial to breaking the influence and power of the enemy over the nations. When God's people are in unity and tightly clinging to the Lord as one body, any one of us can put to flight a thousand of the enemy because the power of God works mightily where there is unity and love for God and for each other. We each must do our best to live and walk in unity for the sake of the kingdom of God.

THE POWER OF ALL

> Behold, how good and pleasant it is when brothers dwell in unity! It is like the precious oil on the head, running down on the beard, on the beard of Aaron, running down on the collar of his robes! It is like the dew of Hermon, which falls on the mountains of Zion! For there the LORD has commanded the blessing, life forevermore. (Psalm 133:1–3 ESV)

Where there is unity, the Lord commands His blessings and life. Unity is what attracts the presence of God and is the driving force behind the power of all. Unfortunately, unity and harmony are not always found in the church. Living in unity and harmony does not mean we all agree on every issue. People will have different opinions, and they are entitled to their opinions; but one thing we all must remember is that God's desire for Christians to work together for the sake of His kingdom is more important than our individual opinions. Most of the things that cause divisions in families, marriages, and churches are rather unimportant. Unity among ourselves as Christians is important because it helps us focus on the vision of God for humanity. It also helps us move in the power of the almighty God.

In 1 Chronicles 29 we see an interesting example of the power of all. King David's son Solomon was chosen by God to be the next king of Israel, but he was young and inexperienced. His first task would be to build the temple of the Lord, but this project was too big for him. Understanding the power of all and also acknowledging that the temple was not for man but for the Lord God, David had led by example by contributing his best gifts toward the building project. And in verse 5 he challenged his people, saying, "Now then, who will follow my example? Who is willing to give offerings to the Lord today?" (NLT). In verse 6 and following, we see the leaders of the households, the leaders of the tribes of Israel, the generals and captains of the army, and the king's administrative officers following the great example of King David by willingly contributing their best gifts to the building project of the house of the Lord.

The people's generosity in giving to the building project not only demonstrated their love for the Lord but also illustrated their united desire to build the house of the Lord. David's great leadership skills and ability to involve his people in building the Lord's house must be praised. No one can successfully build the house of God or bring transformation in the land single-handedly. We need each other.

David's people got involved in the work of building the temple by voluntarily contributing toward the building project. Until we unite and get involved practically in the work of the Lord, using all our resources and spiritual gifts, the church will continue in the same condition it is in. Each individual must willingly give his or her talents, skills, gifts, and resources to the church. God is looking for true leaders like King David who have a passion for His house and are willing to rebuild His house. The problem in the church today is that most leaders are more concerned with building their own reputations and ministries than with building the house of God. Churches of the twenty-first century are busy competing with one another and showing off instead of leading the way in rebuilding the house of the Lord and helping broken communities.

Through unity and the power of all, we can be the channels or vessels God uses in this generation to rebuild the broken house of God and to help the broken-hearted and hurting world. But we can't do this without first reestablishing the boundary stones God set in place from the beginning of time to govern us and give us direction. Those boundary stones, such as the Word of God, the law of God, righteousness, justice, godly love, and honor for God and for each other, have been abandoned, ignored, or moved aside. And we all, like sheep, have gone astray; each one of us has turned to his or her own way. Yet we cannot do without the boundary stones set by God to govern our spiritual lives.

Chapter 10

Reestablishing the Boundary Stones of Our Lives

There are some boundary stones in our lives, in the world, and in the community of believers that should never be moved or tampered with. Unfortunately, however, man has taken his fight for "freedom" to the point of fighting God's established and ordained order for human life. Political leaders, secular leaders, and even a handful of religious leaders around the globe have been pushing to set aside some biblical boundary stones, or principles, God set up to govern human life. Moving the boundary stones God established has led people into bondage, wickedness, and misery. A lawless society or community does not lead people to freedom but to humanitarian disaster. People hate God's law (teaching), but they forget that having His law in place helps to bring order, peace, and stability in the community. God is not a neglectful father; He has set in place the boundary stone of His Word as the governing authority for our lives. To live outside or without the governing authority of the Word of God is simply to live without the breath of our Creator. Life without the Life-giver is worthless and meaningless.

The Word of God is a boundary stone that helps us to live within the secure realm and guidance of God. To live outside God's provided guidance is suicidal. Today most people are living without the wisdom and guidance of God's boundary marker of the Word of God. His Word has been rejected or polluted and diluted with the doctrines and traditions of man.

In this chapter we are going to look at reestablishing the boundary stones of our lives. Proverbs 29:18 tells us, “Without revelation [divine guidance] people run wild, but one who keeps the law will be happy.” Divine guidance, or revelation, refers to the Word of God. Where there is rejection of the Word of God, crime and wickedness run rampant. Without the Word of God, God’s people are powerless. The Word of God is the primary boundary stone for our lives, and it also sets forth all those principles of divine justice, righteousness, and love that also act as boundary stones in our relationship with God and our fellow human beings.

> Do not move an ancient boundary stone, or take over the fields of the fatherless. (Proverbs 23:10 NET)

What is a boundary stone? A boundary stone is a stone that is used to mark off the land. In chapters 13–21 of the book of Joshua, we see how the Promised Land was to be divided among the tribes of Israel. The boundaries were marked out so that each tribe knew exactly where its portion of the land began and ended. Moses warned the people not to cheat their neighbors by moving the boundary stones in order to give themselves more land.

> When you arrive in the land the LORD your God is giving you as a special possession, never steal someone’s land by moving the boundary markers your ancestors set up to mark their property. (Deuteronomy 19:14 NLT)

As the Creator of the heavens, the earth, the sea, and everything that is within them, God knows what is good for His people and what is not good. As such, for our own good, He has established boundaries within which we are to function.

After God placed Adam in the garden of Eden to tend it and watch over it, He told Adam he could freely eat from the fruit of every tree in the garden but one. He gave Adam a limit, or boundary. Adam was not to eat from the Tree of the Knowledge of Good and Evil (Genesis 2:15–17). We all know what Adam and Eve did (Genesis 3). They gave in to Satan’s seduction; they “moved” the “boundary stone” of God’s instruction and ate the fruit from the forbidden tree. The fruit of the tree looked very beautiful and delicious, but it was not good for the spiritual well-being of mankind.

Most of the wisdom and things of this world that are so shiny and attractive lead to spiritual death. Many people today are spiritually dead because they have crossed over the boundary stone of God's teaching and embraced the shiny, attractive gospel of man, a gospel that is centered on idolatry of some type, or materialism, or self-satisfaction and not on the good news of the kingdom of God. The gospel of Jesus Christ is the only gospel that can set the captives free, mend the broken-hearted, and give sight to the spiritually blind.

The rise in violence, lawlessness, and wickedness in the world today is due to the absence of the Word of God. Where there is no divine instruction, there is no fear of God; and where there is no fear of God, there is no honor for God; and where there is no honor and respect for God, there is no respect for human life. When obeyed, God's instruction is a great boundary stone that helps the church and our marriages, relationships, and businesses to function within the character and nature of God. That means we live and do things according to the instructions and power of the Spirit of God. Wickedness and lawlessness can be reversed by reestablishing the Word of God in our lives and in our nation as the governing authority. Teachers, pastors, and evangelists must focus on teaching God's Word and helping people and communities come back to God through the power of His Word. It is the Word of God that has the power and ability to bring change and transformation to this broken and unstable world.

To turn away from the Word of God is simply to turn away from God Himself. John 1:1 tells us, "In the beginning was the Word, and the Word was with God, and the Word was God." The Word of God represents God and His creative power. Creation cannot exist or survive without the breath of God's Word. Psalm 33:6 says, "The heavens were made by the word of the LORD and all the stars, by the breath of His mouth." To live without the Word of God is like trying to live life without oxygen. The church and God's people are spiritually dead when the spiritual oxygen, the Word of God, has been lost. In context John 1:1 is clearly speaking of

Jesus as the Word who was in the beginning with God and was God and became human and made His home among us. So to live our lives without the "Word" of God is simply to live without God and His presence. The Word of God is strongly connected to the power of God. To have the Word of God is to have the power of God.

We are living at a time when many, many people are being led away from God by leaders who are preaching "other gospels" and not the true gospel Jesus preached (cf. Galatians 1:6-9). Their messages sound good, but they make people spiritually weak and unstable and cause many to lose their desire and thirst for God and the things of God. All Christian leaders must remember that the words that come from their mouths have the power to bring people closer to God or to lead them away from God. What connects people to God is not anybody's wisdom, eloquent speaking ability, or authority but the power of the living Word of God. The Word of God is not only the boundary stone of our lives but also the foundation upon which we can securely build our lives. Leaders and all Christians have a big role to play in bringing transformation to this wicked and spiritually dying world. It is important to understand that transformation, reformation, or revival can be achieved only by the power of the Word of God. The world may seem to be hopeless and wicked, but one word from the mouth of God can turn the situation around.

In 2 Kings we see that even the majority of the kings who ruled the southern kingdom of Judah led the people away from worshiping Yahweh, the God of Israel, by turning them away from God's instructions (Word). As a result, the people turned to worshiping idols. Prophet after prophet warned the people that the judgment of God was at hand because of their idolatry, but the people would not repent, or turn back to God. King Manasseh (2 Kings 21:1–18) built pagan altars in the temple of the Lord, even though the Lord had said, "Jerusalem is where I will put My name" (21:4). He even sacrificed his own son in the fire as an offering to a false god. It is recorded that the people did more evil during the reign of Manasseh than had the nations the Lord destroyed before the Israelites (21:9). After Manasseh's death, his son Amon became king in his place and continued the cycle of evil by following completely the ways of his father, worshiping idols and bowing down to them (21:19–26). He did not learn from the mistakes of his father but ignored God and did not walk in obedience to Him. Amon's own servants assassinated him, and his eight-year-old son, Josiah, became king in his place (21:23–24).

TURNING BACK TO GOD THROUGH HIS WORD

Josiah was a different kind of king. He did not follow the ways of his father or build his kingship on the foundation his father Amon or grandfather Manasseh had left. He wanted to change the history of his family and of the nation of Israel by returning to the one and only true, living God of Israel and restoring the house of the Lord. The highlight of his kingship, however, was when the book of the law (God's instructions or teaching) was found in the Lord's temple.

> Then Shaphan the court secretary told the king, "Hilkiah the priest has given me a book," and Shaphan read it in the presence of the king. When the king heard the words of the book of the law, he tore his clothes. Then he commanded Hilkiah the priest, Ahikam son of Shaphan, Achbor son of Micaiah, Shaphan the court secretary, and the king's servant Asaiah: "Go and inquire of the LORD for me, the people, and all Judah about the instruction in this book that has been found. For great is the LORD's wrath that is kindled against us because our ancestors have not obeyed the words of this book in order to do everything written about us." (2 Kings 22:10–13)

When Josiah heard the Word of God, he tore his clothes in despair and immediately instituted reforms throughout the nation (2 Kings 23:4–20). He commanded that the articles made for Baal be removed from the Lord's temple and burned. He did away with the idolatrous priests; he tore down the high places; and he removed all the shrines of the high places, the mediums, the spiritists, the household idols and images, and all the detestable things that were found in the land of Judah and in Jerusalem. The Bible records that before Josiah there was "no king like him who turned to the Lord with all his mind and with all his heart and with all his strength according to all the law of Moses, and no one like him arose after him" (23:25). With just one reading of the Word of God, Josiah was burning with a passion and zeal for the Lord. He willingly responded to the Word of God by bringing reformation throughout the nation. During his reign, Josiah eradicated idolatry from the land and led the people back to God.

THE POWER OF THE WORD OF GOD

There is only one way a nation or people can turn back to God and experience reformation or revival. It is not by man's strategy, skills, or programs but by the power of the living Word of God. John 1:1 tells us, "In the beginning was the Word, and the Word was with God, and the Word was God." And then verse 14 says, "The Word became flesh and took up residence among us. We observed His glory, the glory as the One and Only Son from the Father, full of grace and truth."The "Word" is Jesus Christ. He was in the beginning with God and was God and became human and made his home among us. It is through the power of the living "Word," Jesus Christ, that a nation and people can turn back to God and experience His presence. He is the way, and the truth, and the life; no one comes to the Father except through Him (John 14:6).

If we Christians want to be revived and to see nations come to the Lord, we need to return to Jesus Christ and the written Word of God that reveals Him to us. That means we preach the Word, teach the Word, obey the Word, speak the Word, and live the Word of God. Nothing but the gospel of Jesus Christ has the power to transform our lives or the lives of those around us. As we establish God's Word as our boundary stone, we also reestablish the biblical principles of righteousness, holiness, and justice in our lives, which also act as boundary stones and are clearly set forth in His Word, the Bible.

The church is corrupt and experiencing the same problems as the world because we have moved the boundary stone of our lives. Bring the Word of God back into your marriage, business, relationships, and every aspect of your life, and you shall see the glory and power of the living God. His

Word will illuminate your life and eliminate the forces of darkness that try to disturb or suffocate the life and peace of God in you. The power of the Word of God cannot be emphasized enough. Hebrews 4:12 tells us, "For the word of God is living and effective and sharper than any two-edged sword, penetrating as far as to divide soul, spirit, joints, and marrow; it is a judge of the ideas and thoughts of the heart." The Word of God is living, life giving, and life changing. It reveals who we are and what we are not. It is able to penetrate into the deepest, innermost part of our being to convict us and to change us.

Chapter 11

Revisiting the Foundation of Our Faith and Love for God

In the last chapter we dealt with the importance of reestablishing the boundary stones of our lives. The boundary stones of the Word of God, righteousness, holiness, and justice are not to be moved or tampered with. They are crucial to our spiritual effectiveness and to the well-being of the community of believers. When the Word of God is brought back into our lives as our governing authority, it will be easy for us to walk in the righteousness, holiness, and justice of Jesus Christ. Above all, the Word of God in us is able to help us stay faithful to God and love Him for who He is. In this chapter we are going to revisit the foundation of our faith in God. In so doing, we will discover the depth of true faith in God that will change the motive behind our faith in God and love for Him.

Why do you love God? Why do you worship God? Why do you fear God? And why do you believe in God? These are very important questions we all must answer with an honest heart. When we look at modern Christianity, it is not difficult to tell that for most Christians their faith in God and love for Him are deeply rooted in the fear of going to hell or the desire for prosperity, good health, or healing. In most cases, people come to the Lord out of a "need" and not out of love for who God is. It is not bad to come to the Lord because of our needs or fear of going to hell, but it is shallow and dangerous to base our love for God on physical blessings or the fear of going to hell. Such things should never be the anchors of our relationship with God. God must be loved, honored, exalted, glorified, and worshiped because of His love and unmerited favor toward us.

THE FOUNDATION OF OUR LOVE FOR GOD

> Love consists in this: not that we loved God, but that He loved us and sent His Son to be the propitiation for our sins. . . . There is no fear in love; instead, perfect love drives out fear, because fear involves punishment. So the one who fears has not reached perfection in love. We love because He first loved us. (1 John 4:10, 18–19)

The fear of the final judgment, or eternal punishment, should never be the base or the driving force of our faith and love for God. Our love for God should be centered on God's indescribable love and mercy for us sinners. He demonstrated His love for us by sending Christ to die in our place for our sins. His love for humanity compelled Him to send His only begotten Son, so that everyone who believes in Him should not perish but have everlasting life (John 3:16). He has rescued us from the power of sin and death, He loved us while we were still sinners, He is our Creator and extraordinary Father, and His mercy toward us is priceless. Why not love Him simply for who He is and because of His love for us? The only fear we are to have for God is reverential respect and honor for His holy name. We are going to look more into that when we look at the "fear of the Lord" in chapter 12. True children of God will seek, love, and honor God with or without money, prosperity, or healing because God is far more important in their lives than any worldly and perishable goods. Jesus said, "[God] will give you all you need from day to day if you live for him and make the Kingdom of God your primary concern" (Matthew 6:33 NLT).

> I have been young and now I am old, yet I have not seen the righteous abandoned or his children begging for bread. (Psalm 37:25)

God is faithful; He can never let us down or forsake us. When we take care of His business and seek after Him, He will take care of us. He has no problem prospering us, but if we don't have Him in our lives as our anchor, prosperity will do us more harm than good. We have mentioned Job before, but consider him again as a good example of what it means to truly have faith in and love for God. Job was a prosperous farmer who lived in the land of Uz. He had thousands of sheep and camels and many servants, as well as a large family. He was a man of perfect integrity who feared God and turned away from evil. The Bible records that he was the greatest man among all the people of the east (Job 1:1–3). In fact, God actually considered him the greatest man in all the earth (1:8). God was delighted in His servant Job, but one day the accuser, Satan, came before God, claiming that Job feared God only because of God's hedge of protection around him, his household, and everything he owned. Satan challenged God to stretch out His hand and strike everything Job owned and see if Job would not curse God (1:11). Satan was challenging two things in his accusation of Job: Job's faith in God and God's faith in His servant Job.

God then permitted Satan to touch everything that belonged to Job but not Job himself. Satan destroyed everything Job had, including his children, but Job continued to fear God. This proved that His love for and fear of God were not centered on his properties but rather on the person of God. Seeing that Job still feared God and did not curse God or blame God for anything, Satan said to God, "A man will give up everything he has to save his life. But take away his health, and he will surely curse you to your face!" (Job 2:4–5 NLT). God then allowed Satan to attack Job physically, though He would not permit him to take Job's life. So Satan infected Job with terrible boils from the sole of his foot to the top of his head. Seeing Job suffering in this terrible condition, his wife said to him, "Do you still retain your integrity? Curse God and die!" (2:9). Job replied to her, "You speak as a foolish woman speaks. . . . Should we accept only good from God and not adversity?" (2:10).

Again, Job did not sin against God. He kept his strong moral principles and feared God even in the most traumatic time of his life. Satan wanted to prove to God that the motive behind Job's fear of and love for God was only God's blessings upon him, but Job proved Satan wrong. Job loved God because God is God and worthy of love. Job also proved to humanity that it is possible to love God for who He is, not simply for what He gives. Job's suffering was a great test, not only for Job but for all of us too. The question is this: Can we faithfully love and fear God in the most traumatic times of our lives? Sadly, when they don't see God's blessings or intervention in life's difficulties, many people turn away from God and blame Him for their problems. Prosperity or good health should never determine our loyalty or faithfulness to God. God must be loved regardless of the situations in our lives. Because of Job's faithfulness and determination to remain loyal to God, God restored Job's prosperity and doubled his previous possessions. God is more than sufficient; He is all we need.

It is dangerous to base your relationship with God on His blessings. If you do and then you don't receive what you desire from God, you will lose your hope, trust, and faith in Him. You will question not only His power or ability to do extraordinary things but also His very existence and love for you.

The foundation of our faith and our love for God must be God Himself and not His blessings. The message of prosperity spreading around the world today has transformed believers in Christ into consumer-minded people who are interested only in financial miracles and not in Jesus Christ, the Miracle Worker. Many in the Christian world today are chasing after "prophets" who will lead them into a financial breakthrough, forgetting that every breakthrough actually comes from Jesus Christ. In some parts of the world, people even seek to acquire things by means of witchcraft in order to prove to people or friends that the "Lord" has blessed them. It is not by material things that we prove to people that God has blessed us; it is by walking faithfully in the character and nature of Jesus Christ.

There is nothing wrong with prosperity itself, however. In fact, we need God to prosper us so that we can advance His kingdom here on earth and touch the nations with the power of the gospel of Jesus Christ. Prosperity isn't bad, but the motive behind the desire for it can be very wrong. If our motive is to feed a materialistic desire for more and better and more expensive things, we end up turning God into a moneymaking industry in which everything is centered on what God can do for us and not on what we can do for the kingdom of God through the resurrection power of Jesus Christ.

When Israel was scared of facing Goliath, the young David took it upon himself to do something and defend the name of the God of Israel. Put your faith in God because God is not a man that He should lie or change His mind; He speaks and He acts and He fulfills His promises (Numbers 23:19). If He has commanded us to seek after Him first and promised that if we do so all our needs will be supplied, we must trust His Word. He will bless us; there is no doubt about that.

The foundation for our love for God is God Himself. He is the reason we worship, praise, glorify, and pray to Him. We don't do these things because of our needs but because of who He is. In the same way, we don't walk in faith because we want God to do something for us but because God alone, the Creator of the universe, can be trusted. Faith is not merely a means of obtaining things from God; faith is for walking in and with God regardless of our life situation. Faith is not for selfish gain; faith is for believing in the unchanging character and powerful nature of God.

THE FOUNDATION OF OUR FAITH IN GOD

The foundation of true faith in God is deeply rooted in who God is, not in what we want God to do for us. True faith believes in God whether God does something for us immediately or not. Many people have become disappointed with God because they put their faith in God in order to obtain something from Him; and when God didn't come through for them, they turned their backs on Him. We have looked at Shadrach, Meshach, and Abednego before as wonderful examples of men who had a strong spiritual foundation. Let us consider them again as men who demonstrated what true faith and love for God Almighty is. Because they refused to bow down before the gold statue King Nebuchadnezzar had set up for all the people to worship, the king threatened them, saying, "If you don't worship it, you will immediately be thrown into a furnace of blazing fire—and who is the god who can rescue you from my power?" (Daniel 3:15).

In the face of such a threat, a person with an "ordinary" faith would quickly give in to the pressure of worshiping a man-made god and forsake God Almighty (El Shaddai) to save his or her life from the furnace of blazing fire. When you have a "consumer" kind of faith, a faith that believes in God only for what you can obtain from Him, you can easily give up on God when the going gets tough and you feel like God's presence is not with you. Shadrach, Meshach, and Abednego had an extraordinary faith in God. They responded to the king's threats, saying, "If the God we serve exists, then He can rescue us from the furnace of blazing fire, and He can rescue us from the power of you, the king. But even if He does not rescue us, we want you as king to know that we will not serve your gods or worship the gold statue you set up" (Daniel 3:17–18).

A person with an extraordinary faith does not walk by sight but by faith in God's character and nature. Faith is not based on what is visible but on the invisible God and His faithfulness to do what He has promised to do in our lives when we seek after His kingdom and put Him first above everything else. Shadrach, Meshach, and Abednego had put God first—even before their own lives—and God responded to their faithfulness and trust in Him by delivering them from the fire (Daniel 3:24–27).

The fire had zero effect on their bodies, on their hair, or on their robes because God's presence was with them. King Nebuchadnezzar had no option but to give praise to the only true God. In fact, he issued this decree:

> Anyone of any people, nation, or language who says anything offensive against the God of Shadrach, Meshach, and Abednego will be torn limb from limb and his house made a garbage dump. For there is no other god who is able to deliver like this. (Daniel 3:29)

Many Christians' faith in God is shallow because it is anchored on what they can see and touch with their hands. But the invisible God can be trusted even before we see His power manifested in our lives.

> Now faith is the reality of what is hoped for, the proof of what is not seen. For our ancestors won God's approval by

> it. By faith we understand that the universe was created by God's command, so that what is seen has been made from things that are not visible. (Hebrews 11:1–3)

True faith in God is beyond what we can see or touch, and it is beyond our intellectual capacity and reasoning power. Faith is a conviction that comes through hearing the Word of God and believing the creator God without any doubt, even when our life is at stake. The Greek word translated faith (*pistis*) means intellectual acceptance and conviction of what is true. *Pistis* often is used to translate the Hebrew word *emunah,* which literally means "firm," or securely fixed in place.

Faith in God is securely fixed on the foundation of God's righteousness and love for justice. Faith means having a firm belief in the Word of God and in God's ability and power to do extraordinary things on our behalf. Because God is a righteous God and He loves justice, we need to stand firm on His Word and act upon it. In Hebrew thought, having faith in God is not simply knowing God exists or knowing He will act; rather, it is acting with firmness in regard to God's will. It is God's will to heal, it is God's will to set the captives free, and it is God's will to mend the broken-hearted.

True faith is not based on reasoning or intellect but is fixed on the nature of God. To see the power of God in your life, you need to move away from an intellectual kind of faith (mental faith) into a "firm" and unshakable faith. Unshakable faith is the kind of faith that firmly believes God even when the situation seems hopeless. Whether God answers our prayers or not, our faith in Him must be firmly secure in who God is. God is God. He never changes; and because we have His DNA in us, we also must not change our love toward Him, even in the most difficult times of our lives. Even if we lose a family member, a job, or a business, genuine faith in God will still remain intact. He is our foundation of solid rock, and no circumstance can shake our faith and trust in Him. Faith in God and in who He is can take us to a place where our intelligence, skills, ability, and wisdom cannot take us. Faith in God can turn a weak person into a strong and powerful warrior of God.

It is essential that you build your faith on the nature of God because Satan's strategy is to attack the foundation of your faith in God and plant in you seeds of unbelief, fear, and doubt so that he can disconnect you from God's presence and God's promises. Let God be the center of your love, and let the Devil know that you love God, not because of His blessings but because of who He is. Use your faith to honor God, and God will honor your faith and faithfulness. Faith in the nature of God will cause you to walk in the fear of the Lord and honor His holy name.

The spirit of unbelief is very dangerous. Not only does it lead a person to doubt God, but it also leads one to disrespect God and become too familiar with Him. The lack of honor for the living God in the community of believers today is due to the spirit of unbelief. Faith will lead you to worship God with excellency, but the spirit of unbelief will cause you to worship God anyway *you* choose. By faith Abel offered to God a more excellent sacrifice than Cain (Hebrews 11:4). Abel's faith in God led him to bring an honorable sacrifice before God.

Chapter 12

Familiarity With God: A Disease of the Heart

What does "familiarity" with God mean? The word *familiarity* indicates a close acquaintance with someone or the quality of being well known. It conveys the sense of relaxed friendliness and the absence of fences experienced in knowing someone very well. By familiarity with God we simply mean knowing God well enough and in such a way as to lose a sense of the awe, respect, and honor for Him that He deserves. For example, when Jesus, the King of kings and the Son of the living God, visited His hometown in Mark 6:1–6, the people there, instead of giving Him honor and rejoicing that He was now in their midst, treated Him with the spirit of familiarity. They said, "He's just a simple carpenter, the son of Mary and the brother of James, Joseph, Judas, and Simon. And His sisters live right here among us." The people of Jesus' hometown were offended by the acclaim He was receiving. They refused to believe in Jesus Christ because they were too familiar with Him, as well as with His family. To them He was just a common person and nothing special. Familiarity with God can cause a person to view God as common and to treat Him with contempt.

In Mark 6:4 Jesus told the people, "A prophet is honored everywhere except in his own hometown and among his relatives and his own family" (NLT). Jesus was well known to those of His hometown, and this was why they could not fathom the idea that He was the promised Messiah.

Because they were too familiar with Jesus, unbelief filled their hearts; and Jesus could not do any mighty miracles among them except to heal a few sick people. He was amazed by the magnitude of their unbelief. Even in our communities today, people struggle to accept, honor, or receive the message of God from a person they have known very well since childhood. Being too familiar with God is dangerous because it can prevent us from receiving God's anointing, revelation, and gifting.

SIGNS OF FAMILIARITY WITH GOD

> "A son honors his father, and a servant his master. But if I am a father, where is My honor? And if I am a master, where is your fear of Me? says Yahweh of Hosts to you priests, who despise My name." Yet you ask: "How have we despised Your name?" "By presenting defiled food on My altar." You ask: "How have we defiled You?" When you say: "The LORD's table is contemptible." "When you present a blind animal for sacrifice, is it not wrong? And when you present a lame or sick animal, is it not wrong? Bring it to your governor! Would he be pleased with you or show you favor?" asks the LORD of Hosts. "And now ask for God's favor. Will He be gracious to us? Since this has come from your hands, will He show any of you favor?" asks the LORD of Hosts. "I wish one of you would shut the temple doors, so you would no longer kindle a useless fire on My altar! I am not pleased with you," says the LORD of Hosts, "and I will accept no offering from your hands." (Malachi 1:6–10)

Malachi, the last Old Testament prophet, who preached about 430 BC, rebuked the people and the priests for becoming too familiar with God and thus neglecting His worship and failing to honor His name. The people had lost their passion for worship, which led to apathy and disillusionment because the messianic prophecies of Jeremiah, Isaiah, and Micah had not yet been fulfilled. God had commanded genuine worship with wholehearted faith and humility, which included honoring Him with pure offerings. However, the people willfully chose to disobey God's commands by offering Him defiled sacrifices. Instead of leading the way in honoring and fearing the Lord, the priests also became too familiar with God and led the people into sin (Malachi 2:7–9). The hearts of the people became hardened by sin, which led them to be unfaithful and to break their covenant with God. The nation of Israel in that day struggled to faithfully follow God because of the hardness of their hearts. Hardness of heart is what produces the spirit of familiarity with God. When a person's heart is hardened toward God and His Word, the end result is detachment from God's instruction and life. The heart, as we have already discussed, is the spiritual engine of our relationship with God.

In Jeremiah 31:31–33 we find God's declaration:

> "The time is coming," declares the LORD, "when I will make a new covenant with the house of Israel and with the house of Judah. It will not be like the covenant I made with their forefathers when I took them by the hand to lead them out of Egypt, because they broke my covenant, though I was a husband to them," declares the LORD. "This is the covenant I will make with the house of Israel after that time," declares the LORD. "I will put my law in their minds and write it on their hearts. I will be their God, and they will be my people." (NIV)

The problem with the old covenant was not with God or the contents of the covenant; rather, the problem was with the hearts of God's people, who broke their covenant with God (Jeremiah 11:10). Honor and respect for God comes from the heart. When your heart is sold out for God, you will honor His name and bring the best sacrifice of worship to Him; but when your heart is corrupt, you don't care about honoring the name of God or bringing the best sacrifice to Him. In Matthew 15:8 Jesus quoted the words of Isaiah the prophet, who said, "These people honor me with their lips, but their hearts are far away" (NLT). The religious leaders of Jesus' day knew a lot about God, but they didn't honor God. They claimed to honor Him, but their hearts were far from Him.

The message of Malachi to the nation of Israel in his day is very important for a generation like ours, which has grown too familiar with God and has little sense of honor or reverence for the Lord. If God is indeed our Father and Master, where is the honor for His name in our lives? Honoring God wholeheartedly attracts His presence and power. If we want to see the power of God's presence manifested in our lives, we need to give honor to His name, His house, and His servants (pastors). We are not seeing miracles in the church today because we have become too familiar, not only with God, but also with each other. How can we move in the power of the gifts or anointing of God that is upon each one of us if we don't honor and respect God and each other? Romans 12:10 commands us to love each other with genuine affection and to take delight in honoring each other.

One of the clearest signs of the spirit of familiarity with God is a lack of honor and respect for God's Word, house, leaders, and children. Avoiding the spirit of familiarity with God and with each other should be every Christian's goal and desire. If we don't resist the spirit of familiarity with God in our hearts, our hearts will grow cold toward the leading of the Spirit of God. Familiarity with God can cause us to lose respect for the Lord and for His chosen leaders. Familiarity with God prevents the Holy Spirit from working effectively both in the church and in the lives of individual Christians.

To a believer, familiarity with God is valuable only as it pertains to the principles of God, which never change. In being "familiar" with God's principles, we avoid a sinful lifestyle, we give honor and glory to His name, we respect the leaders He has placed over us, we respect other believers regardless of their background, race, or nationality, we respect the house of the Lord, we walk in the fear of the Lord, we love God wholeheartedly and love others, and we honor God with our resources, money (tithes and offerings), and time. By being familiar with the principles of God, we obey His Word and live according to His will.

THE DANGERS OF BEING TOO FAMILIAR WITH GOD

In Leviticus 10:1–4 we see the dangers of being too familiar with God.

> Aaron's sons Nadab and Abihu put coals of fire in their incense burners and sprinkled incense over it. In this way, they disobeyed the LORD by burning before him a different kind of fire than he had commanded. So fire blazed forth from the LORD's presence and burned them up, and they died there before the LORD. Then Moses said to Aaron, "This is what the LORD meant when he said, 'I will show myself holy among those who are near me. I will be glorified before all the people.'" And Aaron was silent. Then Moses called for Mishael and Elzaphan, Aaron's cousins, the sons of Aaron's uncle Uzziel. He said to them, "Come and carry the bodies of your relatives away from the sanctuary to a place outside the camp." (NLT)

Aaron's descendants were chosen by God to serve Him as priests. The special gifts presented to the Lord by the Israelites had been reserved for Aaron and his descendants from the time they were set apart to serve the Lord as priests (Leviticus 7:34–36). Aaron's sons, Nadab and Abihu, offered fire before the Lord that was contrary to His commands. The crime of Nadab and Abihu was not the incense but rather offering the fire to God in their own way instead of in a way permitted by God (Exodus 30:9). By acting in this way, they violated the holiness of God and His instruction. It was dishonoring to God for Nadab and Abihu to offer strange or foreign fire to Him. God responded by killing them instantly.

While today God may not instantly kill us for breaking His instruction or violating His holiness, as He killed Nadab and Abihu, He will withdraw His presence and power from among us (Psalm 51:11). The danger of being too familiar with God is that we can easily lose a sense of deep admiration for God. In addition, we can begin to think we are following the leading of the Holy Spirit by doing certain things "for God" when God's heart is not in it. The spirit of familiarity with God can hinder our spiritual growth and the work of God in our lives. By all means, as children of the most holy God, we must guard our hearts from the spirit of familiarity with God and be sensitive to His Holy Spirit. And we need to develop and exhibit a lifestyle that honors God, pastors, and fellow Christians.

Conclusion

It is very important to understand that behind every social and spiritual problem stands the greater problem of the foundation. The foundation of our life is the source of our spiritual strength and stability. We cannot withstand or overcome the demonic forces of this world without building a strong spiritual foundation. Men and women of God have tried to transform, reform, or change society with little success because their focus has been on the symptoms of the problem and not on the foundational disease. Transformation of a society or community of believers is achieved only by dealing with the root cause of the problem: the foundation. The foundation, or "heart," is the source of sinful attitudes and behavior. God's focus is on the human heart. He is on a mission of transforming the hearts of those who are willing and desirous of walking with Him. We can't claim to walk with God or to be a revived people if our hearts are far from God and full of envy, jealousy, hatred, unforgiveness, and bitterness.

In the Hebrew Scriptures (Old Testament), we see that the main problem the chosen people of God had throughout history was hardness of heart. Through His prophet Jeremiah, the Lord said to the sinful and idolatrous people of Judah, "The heart is more deceitful than anything else and desperately sick—who can understand it? I, the LORD, examine the mind, I test the heart to give to each according to his way, according to what his actions deserve" (Jeremiah 17:9–10). Judah's problem was the nation's foundation. Wicked kings such as Manasseh and Amon had laid a foundation of idolatry. The people would not turn away from worshiping idols to worshiping the one and only true God because the spirit of idols had captured their hearts. King Josiah's reformation could not totally overcome the effect of the evil foundation Manasseh and Amon had laid down. Only with a new heart would the people be able to turn away from idol worship and turn to God. And in Jeremiah 24:7 God promised to give His people a new heart: "I will give them a heart to know Me, that I am the LORD. They will be My people, and I will be their God because they will return to Me with all their heart."

THE GOOD SOIL

The church today is weak and sick because of the hardness of our hearts toward God and toward His Word. Our hearts have been corrupted by the things of this world to the point that we can't respond to the power of God's Word. It is not God's fault that we are not seeing His miraculous power in our lives. As a matter of fact, God wants to walk in our midst and He has been walking among us through His Holy Spirit, but we can't even feel or sense His presence because the worries and things of this world have captured our hearts. The hardness of our hearts prevents us from walking in the tangible power of God, bearing godly fruit, and forcefully advancing the kingdom of God.

In Matthew 13:1–9 Jesus told a parable about a farmer who went out to sow. As he was sowing, some seeds fell along the path, and the birds came and ate them up. Others fell on rocky ground, where there was not much soil. Plants sprang up quickly from the seeds, but the soil was not deep; so when the sun came up, the plants were scorched, and since they had no roots, they withered. Other seeds fell among thorns, and the thorns came up and choked them. Still others fell on good ground and produced a crop—some one hundred, some sixty, and some thirty times what was sown.

It is very clear that in the parable the sower represents Jesus, who went forth and scattered seeds (the good news of the kingdom) on four different types of ground and got four different results or responses. The first three grounds did not produce fruit (respond well) because the soil was not good enough to support life. Only the fourth ground was good and produced the fruit.

Jesus' emphasis in the parable of the sower was on the various types of soil. The seed (Word of God) was good, but the quality of the soils varied. The kind of soil in which a farmer plants his seed will determine the growth of his crops. If the soil is good, the seed will take root and produce good and healthy crops; but if the soil is not good, the seed will produce nothing. Usually when a farmer puts his seed into the ground and nothing comes up, it is not the seed's fault but the ground's (soil). The seed (Word of God) Jesus has planted and continues to plant through men and women of God is good, but the soil, which is the human heart, isn't good.

Jesus' explanation of the parable of the sower highlights four different responses to the Word of God as portrayed by the different types of soil. The hard ground represents people who have hardened their hearts toward the Word of God. They hear His Word but do not understand it, and Satan plucks the message away, keeping their hearts dull and preventing the Word from making an impression. The stony ground pictures those who initially profess delight with the Word. However, their hearts are not changed; and when trouble arises, their so-called faith quickly disappears. The thorny ground depicts people who seem to receive the Word but whose hearts are full of the love of riches, pleasures, and the things of this world. These things take their time and attention away from the Word, and they end up having no time for it. The good ground portrays those who hear, understand, and receive the Word—and then allow the Word to accomplish its result in their lives.

The parable of the sower can help us realize the importance of having a good soil (foundation). In the context of our study, the hard, stony, and thorny grounds represent a bad foundation, while the good ground represents a good foundation. With a good foundation we can hear, understand, receive, and respond to the Word of God and produce godly fruit. We must focus on laying a good foundation with the Word of God in our lives and in the hearts of the forthcoming generation if we are to turn the nations from wickedness to God.

THE STRONG FOUNDATION

We have spent considerable time in this book explaining the need for a strong spiritual foundation. Without such a foundation, we are doomed to sway or even collapse when the storms of life come. We will be empty, frustrated, and defeated spiritually. A strong spiritual foundation is essential if we are to live victoriously in this life, free from the power of sin and able to serve and honor God effectively.

A strong spiritual foundation has at its base the foundation of Jesus Christ. When we are saved through faith in Christ, He becomes the one true and tested bedrock foundation for our lives. Our lives are not suddenly perfected when we trust in Christ, for our spiritual foundation is not yet complete. However, we are set on a new path with Christ as our foundation. On the bedrock foundation of Christ, we must build the spiritual foundation that will see us through life successfully. We cannot make the mistake of trying to build on our old life and values or simply adding Christ to the old foundation of our lives. We must leave the past behind and allow God, through His Word and the Holy Spirit, to destroy the old, worldly foundation. We must build upon Christ and the principles He sets forth in His Word.

It is in our hearts, the very center of our being, that the building process takes place. In our hearts we determine to follow Christ and His Word. God supplies Jesus Christ, the Word of God, and the Holy Spirit, but we add to this foundation consistent obedience, reverence (fear), persistent prayer, and ever-growing faith to build a lasting spiritual foundation that will serve us all the days of our lives. God supplies the means and the power; we submit to Him and allow Him to build us up through His Word. The evidence that we have indeed built a strong spiritual foundation is the fruit of the Spirit in our lives.

As we build this spiritual foundation on the foundation of Christ and His Word, we are preparing ourselves to be part of the united, powerful church God is building in this generation. But we must be vigilant for those attitudes that will derail us and move us off our foundation. We need to continually revisit our foundation and be sure we are acknowledging and observing the boundary stones of the Word of God and all it teaches us about righteousness, holiness, justice, and love. We must be sure our faith in and love for God are based, not on His blessings and what we hope to get from Him, but on who God is and what He has already done for us in Christ. A strong and growing faith in God and love for Him must be based on the very nature of God. And, finally, we must revisit our foundation to make sure we are avoiding an attitude of familiarity with God that would jeopardize the spiritual foundation we have built.

Revisit your spiritual foundation today, and embark on a journey of rebuilding your spiritual life by responding to the Word of God with obedience and walking in the character and nature of Jesus Christ. Don't wait for circumstances in life to surprise you; instead, "surprise" every circumstance and challenge in your life by standing unshakably on Christ, the pillar of your life. Let the Devil know you will not give up or give in, no matter how severe your trials may be. In Christ alone you believe, you stand, you move, you breathe, and you have your being. When your spiritual foundation is strong, you will not be shaken. You will follow, honor, serve, and please God, and you will have a powerful impact upon the world.

About the Author

Dr. Kazumba Charles Th.D., is a passionate preacher, Bible teacher, Evangelist, Radio host of Keep The Fire Burning program and the author of the Parables of the kingdom. His messages are life changing, refreshing, motivating, inspiring, and uplifting. His vision and burning desire is to reach millions of people for Jesus Christ, empower men and women to advance the kingdom of God, help orphaned children, and fight HIV/AIDS in Africa.

www.kazumbacharles.com

Printed in the United States
By Bookmasters